DIGITAL REVOLUTIONARIES
WHO HAVE CHANGE THE WORLD

DIGITAL REVOLUTIONARIES Who Have Changed The WORLD

Kalyani Mookherji

Ocean Books Pvt. Ltd.
ISO 9001:2015 Publishers

Published by
Ocean Books (P) Ltd.
4/19 Asaf Ali Road,
New Delhi-110 002 (INDIA)
e-mail: info@oceanbooks.in

ISBN 978-81-8430-523-4
DIGITAL REVOLUTIONARIES WHO HAVE CHANGED THE WORLD
by Kalyani Mookherji

Edition
2025

Price
₹ 500.00 (Rupees Five Hundred only)

Printed at
Yash Printographics, Noida

Introduction

The history of human knowledge is a proof that technology evolves constantly. However some phases of history, more than others, experience a special burst of creativity as various factors like availability of resources, encouragement to research, dissemination of knowledge and individual talent come together. One such recent phase, has been some analysts would argue, is still continuing—is the digital revolution.

Sociology experts have identified the latter half of the twentieth century as marking the birth of the digital revolution when mechanical and analog electronics started giving way to digital electronics. The invention of the transistor, the earliest computing machines, the World Wide Web and its evolution into the internet marked the high points of this part of the digital revolution. These inventions changed the way people worked, studied as well as sought information and of entertainment. More importantly, they could now reach out to anyone and anything in the world through the internet. These inventions transformed entertainment, socializing, commerce, politics and studies in ways that would hardly be conceivable a generation back.

The next major stage in the digital revolution was the arrival of mobile devices, starting with the cellphone in 1973. Eventually this led to the development of tablets and smartphones where a significant feature is the integration with internet as well as online products and services. This has, in turn, opened up the scope for business, networking –

both social and professional – and entertainment as never before.

Not surprisingly a new breed of technology experts and entrepreneurs has sprung up to take advantage of this dynamic new medium. Greatest Digital Revolutionaries offers a brief glimpse into the work, achievements and future plans of some such individuals who have significantly contributed to the fields of ecommerce, information technology and related businesses. The names are alphabetically listed and its selection is determined by no other parameter than the author's own limited awareness. The book is simply a sampler of the better known tech innovators, programmers and entrepreneurs today. They have made a name for themselves by coming up with exciting products and services that not only seek to enhance the quality of life for the contemporary human being but also explore new ideas in sustainable and holistic development of human society.

—Kalyani Mookherji

Contents

1
Alexis Ohanian

Alexis Ohanian is an American internet entrepreneur of Armenian origin who is best known for co-founding social news website 'Reddit' among other online ventures. He is the CEO of Reddit as well as a passionate supporter of free Internet.

Early Life

Alexis was born on April 24, 1983 to Chris and Anke Ohanian. Chris was of Armenian origin and was the descendent of survivors of the Armenian genocide. Anke, on the other hand, was of German origin.

Childhood was full of challenges for Alexis who felt somewhat awkward being the tallest boy in class, slightly overweight and with a name meant for girls in the mainstream American culture. In all this, his computer was his main refuge which he got as a gift from his parents shortly after his tenth birthday. Alexis started enjoying computer even more when his parents provided him with a dial-up internet connection. He began creating websites on his own and realized this is what he wanted to do later in life too. According to his autobiography, one of the most memorable times of his childhood was a part-time job at Sidea where, in-between giving demonstrations on its hardware and software, he got to spend hours surfing the internet.

Alexis graduated from Howard High School in Ellicott City, Maryland and then enrolled in the University of Virginia where he obtained his degrees in commerce and history. Here he also met his future business partner and Reddit co-founder Steve Huffman and bonded over a common love of video games.

Success with Reddit

After leaving college in 2005, Ohanian and Huffman managed to obtain a meeting with Paul Graham of Y Combinatior, a firm which provides seed-funding to startups. Though Graham did not think much of their then business idea—a mobile food ordering service named 'MobileMenu'—he saw the young men's potential and encouraged them to create a website that would grab eyeballs.

For the next three weeks, Ohanian and Huffman worked hard at putting together what would emerge as a social news website. It was essentially a compilation of Web-links and user-submitted text that could be rated as 'Interesting' or 'Uninteresting', with relevant buttons before the news pieces. After a lot of deliberation, the creators agreed to add a "Comments" section, based on their vision of Reddit being a primarily user-based oriented business.

Very soon, Reddit increased in popularity and in 2006, it was lapped up by Condé Nast at a price that has never been exactly disclosed though estimates vary from 10 million to 20 million US dollar. Even after the acquisition, Ohanian remained a Member of its Board of Directors and continued his interest in the site. He later wrote in his biography about the euphoria experienced with the big sale—"As soon as the money came into his checking it, he apparently called Washington Redskins ticket office and upgraded his Dad's tickets to more expensive ones and a little later he made a sizeable donation to a charity that his mother preferred"—by that time she had passed away after suffering from brain tumour.

Newer Ventures

Ohanian left Reddit after three years of the acquisition and travelled to Armenia—his country of origin—on a Kiva fellowship. Among the many ventures he started after Reddit, was 'BreadPig', which sells geeky merchandize online and gives its profits to charity. New ventures and startups continue to be his main interest and he travels extensively across the world, giving talks on encouraging the spirit of entrepreneurship. As part of these endeavours, he has also started radio podcasts. On October 15, 2014, Ohanian launched the NYRD Radio which not only has eminent entrepreneurs as guest speakers but also has a section called 'Office Hours', in which aspiring business owners can apply to develop an idea with him. Yet another such initiative is 'Upvoted', which every week features a meaningful story of a guest from Reddit around whom that story revolves.

However in recent years, another issue has caught the attention of Ohanian—Free Internet. When the Stop Online Piracy Act began to be pushed by the Congress and likewise the Protect IP Act by the Senate, it resulted in heated discussions on Reddit and other online forums. Ohanian then realized that such bills could be actually targeted at every user-generated website. He believed it was really drafted by lobbyists rather than technologists, and by his own admission, "Would have made starting a site like Reddit impossible". In response, Ohanian arrived in Washington DC and began giving interviews to the media on how such a Bill could effectively mean the end of free internet. He was even summoned to testify before the Congress but such was the outpouring of public opinion against the proposed Bills, but before that could happen, the Bills withdrawn.

Ohanian however continued his activism for open internet. In October 2012, accompanied by Reddit, General Manager Erik Martin, he undertook an Internet 2012 Bus Tour from Denver, CO to Danville, KY to raise awareness about these issues during the Presidential and Vice Presidential debates. In recognition of his contribution to the Open Internet Campaign, *The Daily Dot,* named him as the topmost influential activist of 2012, while *Forbes* gave him the nickname of "Mayor of the Internet".

In his personal life too, Alexis Ohanian gives evidence of a wacky and expressive temperament. Believed to be currently dating tennis superstar Serena Williams, he lives in Brooklyn, New York. Ohanian often reveals how uncomfortable he is with excessive restrictions of demeanour, language and behaviour. His free, unhindered personality, according to his supporters, is one of the reasons of his enduring popularity among the younger generations who are in awe of the man who became a millionaire even before he touched 25!

□

2
Andrew Mason

Who doesn't love deals! And for someone always on the lookout for deals, 'Groupon' is a familiar name. This is a web portal that offers heavy discounts to users on local businesses and was co-founded by American internet entrepreneur 'Mason' who was also its CEO. On the basis of his stake in Groupon as well as other ventures, Mason had a current net worth of 200 million US$, as of 2013.

Early Life

Andrew Mason was born on October 22, 1980 in the Pennsylvanian city of Pittsburgh. Both his parents were entrepreneurs—his father was a diamond salesman while his mother owned a photography business. Not surprisingly Mason was a budding entrepreneur early on—when just fifteen, he started 'Bagel Express', a delivery service for bagels on weekends.

However it was his passion for melody and rhythm that determined his college course as he enrolled in Northwestern University to study for a bachelor's degree in music. But after graduating in 2003 he was unable to find work and hence took up a job as a software developer at InnerWorkings Inc. It was here that he met Chicago-based entrepreneur, Eric Lefkosky with whom he would formally start Groupon in 2008.

Success with Groupon

But before that, Mason got an idea to start Point.com, a website that encouraged collective action to support various causes. Apparently the project was started when he faced the problem of terminating his cellular telephone contract. It occurred to Mason that many other people must be facing the same problem and if they could be brought together in an organized plan of action, such problem could be solved. The site grew into a rallying point for users to express their support for a specific cause such as supporting a charity, funding a scholarship or even boycotting a product. Users however were not required to pay any money or give their time to the particular cause until a certain level of interest was attained. It was only when the campaign's "Tipping Point", was reached, that further action would take place. When Mason saw that many of the site's most successful projects brought users together to acquire buying power, he got the idea to spin-off a commercial site on the same logic. This was initially known as 'Getyourgroupon.com' and to launch this, Mason roped in Lefkosky and Keywell. Eventually the site came to be known as 'Groupon.com'—a fusion of the words 'group' and 'coupon' and was properly launched in 2008.

Groupon was designed as a group discount site where users were encouraged to sign up for deals on a variety of products and services which could range from dining out and car tune-ups to spa packages and theatre tickets. Within just seven months of its launch, Groupon turned profitable. By early 2011 more than 30 million offers were claimed by customers using the Group network. As a mark of its phenomenal success, the company decided to raise funding in November 2011 and managed to attract $700 million through its initial public offering which turned out to be the largest by an Internet company since Google Inc.'s $1.66 billion IPO in 2004.

However by 2012 Groupon was struggling to keep up its revenues and by August its stock had fallen by 75 per cent. In February 2013, Mason took responsibility for the company's poor performance and stepped down from the post of CEO to make way for his Groupon co-founder, Lefkosky.

Life after Groupon

After leaving Groupon, Mason took a six month break to get his life back on track. This not only included looking after his health and hence checking into a weight-loss camp in Miami but also looking after his family. Married to pop singer Jenny Gillespie, Mason welcomed a baby during this time and additionally he also recorded an album of motivational business songs.

In February 2015, Mason co-founded 'Detour' that has created an iPhone app for location-based audio walking tours. With this app, a user can listen to audio narratives that give a quirky take on walking tours in a particular city. The app started with San Francisco, where it's based and eventually expanded to include New York, Chicago, Los Angeles and Austin. A subscription to the app costs $20 a year, or a user can buy individual Detours for $5.

Mason points out that Detour is world apart from traditional walking tours which cast the user in a rather passive role of staring at a small screen. According to Mason, Detour on the other hand engages the user much more actively, as though he/she is a character in the narrative. Additionally Mason claims that the app uses a more sophisticated location technology so that the narrative and music are in perfect sync with the user's movements, this removes the need to look at the phone repeatedly.

Detour draws on Mason's passion for music and travel that he has been, evident since the earliest stages of his adult life. But more than that, with this new venture, Mason seeks to give the art of story-telling a fresh breath of life, because, after all, his life and achievements have been nothing short of one amazing story too!

□

3

Arash Ferdowsi

Arash Ferdowsi is an American internet entrepreneur of Iranian origin who is best known for co-founding the cloud based storage service, 'Dropbox'. As of 2015, he enjoyed a net worth of $500 million according to *Forbes*, which also ranked him at the 33rd position on its 2015 List of America's Richest Entrepreneurs under 40.

Early Life

The son of Iranian immigrants, Arash Ferdowsi was born on October 7, 1985 in Overland Park, Kansas. Right from his childhood, young Ferdowsi impressed people with his brilliance, especially with his expertise in computers. In 2004 he finished first in his high school class from Blue Valley Northwest High School and then got through Massachusetts Institute of Technology (MIT). Here he came across another student, Drew Houston, and the two hit off together amidst a common fascination for computers.

While still at MIT, Houston had started developing a cloud based storage service but soon he realized that he would be able to do justice to it only with some help from a partner. In 2007 thus Houston, who had graduated by then, asked Ferdowsi to work with him on the project. Ferdowsi, who was then in his last year of college, was convinced enough to dropout so that he could devote himself full time to Houston's project.

Success with Dropbox

Launched in 2007, Dropbox is a free cloud-based file-syncing service that enables users to access and share their digital files, photos and videos practically from any computer or mobile device.

Initially the company faced the usual round of teething troubles which the founder duo worked tirelessly to solve. For three months, Ferdowsi and Houston would slog away at a cramped office in Cambridge, waking up everyday at noon and working till dawn the next day.

All this hard work seemed to bear fruit when in 2011 the company received a funding of worth 7.2 million USD from Sequoia Capital, Accel Partners, Y Combinator and a bunch of individual investors. This turned out to be an important source of support for the team, enabling them to push on. However their popularity was still low and this proved to be a matter of concern, but all that changed with an instruction video on Digg that showed how to use Dropbox. The video went viral and within just a few hours, their beta waiting list went from 5,000 to 75,000 people. This event made the founders realize the vast potential of Dropbox and how it deserve much more commitment.

While Houston decided to head the management of the company as CEO, Ferdowsi became its Chief Technical Officer (CTO). In his role as the CTO, Ferdowsi is responsible for enhancing the range and quality of products from Dropbox so that it is able to compete against industry giants like Apple, Google and Microsoft. Ferdowsi has also acquired a bit of reputation as a workaholic. Dubbed the "Chief Debugger", he is known to send emails to his employees even at three in the morning when an outage or something similar has to be fixed.

Despite growing success, Ferdowsi and Houston still try to keep things as simple as possible. The company does not spend much on advertising—instead it relies on a referral program that gives users free storage space in exchange of new customers to the site. The major chunk of revenue for Dropbox comes from its premium plans. While the service is free for up to 2 GB of storage, for 50 GB of space the users have to pay 9.99 USD per month and for 100 GB, it is 19.99 USD per month. Dropbox users range from individuals and small enterprises to event-organizers and even large brands like Red Bull. In fact half of the Dropbox users are located outside the United States which in turn has motivated the company to launch the service in languages like Spanish, French, German, and Japanese.

Based in San Francisco, the Dropbox now has more than 500 employees. It acquired popular email app Mailbox in addition to teams from smaller startups like Endorse, Sold and Snapjoy. In 2013 Dropbox hosted a developer's conference for the first time and also brushed its Business Products range in order to attract investors. Since its founding, Dropbox has raised 1.1 billion USD in venture funding, with the most recent roundbeing in January 2014 when it attracted a massive 250 million USD based on a valuation which pegged the company at 10 billion USD. Today, Dropbox boasts of more than 25 million registered users who save over a million files every five minutes.

All this has made Arash Ferdowsi one of the hottest tech entrepreneurs in the Silicon Valley—and that too at the age of just 30. No wonder then that in 2011 TechCrunch awarded Ferdowsi a Crunchie for "Founder Of The Year", while Inc. Magazine listed Ferdowsi as its 2011 "30 Under 30", top entrepreneurs. Again in the same year, *Fortune* Magazine included Ferdowsi in its "40 Under 40", list, which features the forty most outstanding entrepreneurs under the age of forty. In year 2015, *Forbes* ranked Ferdowsi at the 33rd position in its 2015 list of America's Richest Entrepreneurs Under 40.

□

4

Ben Silbermann

If you are an avid netizen, chances are that several times during browsing for images or information, you have visited 'Pinterest'. This exciting pinboard of images and links is the result of the creative genius of Ben Silbermann who is the CEO and co-founder of the site. Today Pinterest is among the top sites around for images and it is largely responsible for Silbermann's net worth of $1.57 billion as of June 2016, when he is just 33 years of age.

Early Life

Silbermann was born in 1982 and raised in Des Moines, Iowa. Both his parents, Jane Wang and Neil Silbermann, are ophthalmologists and still run a family practice based in the city. As a child, one of Silbermann's favourite hobbies was collecting dried insects, which he pinned to cardboard. Later he would credit his childhood interest with being the inspiration behind his extraordinary business success. "Collecting tells a lot about who you are," he once revealed in an interview. And it is this interest that gave him the opportunity for internet success—apparently when planning his startup, he looked at the web and found that "There wasn't a place to share that side of who you were".

While growing up, Silbermann was a brilliant student. In 1998, he attended the Research Science Institute (RSI) at

Massachusetts Institute Technology (MIT) which is a highly competitive summer research program for high school students from around the world. In fact, the RSI is sponsored by the Center for Excellence in Education and hosted by MIT in Cambridge, Massachusetts. Eventually he attended the Des Moines Central Academy and graduated high school from Theodore Roosevelt Academy of Des Moines in 1999.

Initially Silbermann thought of becoming a doctor, like his parents were and like his siblings would go on to become—he even enrolled at Yale as a pre-med student. However a change of heart saw him switching course and in the spring of 2003, he graduated from Yale College with a degree in political science.

Silbermann next moved to Washington DC with a consultancy job. Around this time, he got interested in technology and was especially impressed by the blog, TechCrunch. Following his new-found interest, he left DC for the West Coast where he managed to get a job in Google. His brief was to design and display products like display ads.

After working at AdSense—the online advertising group of Google-for several years, Silbermann once again answered the call of his heart's longings and left. He now wanted to do something of his own. One of his first ventures was the designing of iPhone apps for which he teamed up with a college friend, Paul Sciarra. One of the results of that time was 'Tote' which never really took off.

But Silbermann was not ready to give up just yet. He and Sciarra roped in Evan Sharp, a budding product designer to create an online pinboard where users could 'pin' and save images of their choice as well as share them and rate or 'like' images curated by others. The website was named 'Pinterest' and launched in 2010. Soon after it went live, Silbermann emailed a link to the site to his contacts and 'in fact', it was his friends in Iowa who were the first to pick it up and start using it.

Success with Pinterest

The first year for Pinterest did not prove to be easy. Even after nine months, the site had less than 10,000 users. However while working in the customer support in Google, Silbermann had learnt many important lessons, including reaching out to the clients and keeping them happy. He emailed to the first 5,000 users of Pinterest personally to get their feedback. Gradually the site began to get noticed. In this way, Pinterest engaged the mainstream of users before it engaged the tech crowd, and this has been one of the reasons of its spectacular success. Year 2014, in fact, saw the site growing faster than Facebook and Twitter even.

Another factor has been perhaps the "Scrapbook", idea behind the success Pinterest that was inspired by Silbermann's own childhood hobby of collecting things. While other social media sites like Twitter and Facebook require users to generate their own content, Pinterest lets users "repin" other people's content, as Silbermann believes "Most people don't have anything witty to say on Twitter or any major news to share on Facebook. But everyone can collect stuff".

Silbermann's connection to Pinterest is in fact, deeply personal on more levels than one. For a long time now its most popular pinner has been the CEO's own mother. Jane Wang's page is fun and quirky—with a chinstrap penguin from Antarctica being her profile picture! What's more, she has more than eight million followers though most among these are unaware of her relation to Silbermann. Indeed, her board titled "Delicious", is most popular for all the yummy recipes it has pinned on it.

In 2014, Silbermann finally decided to monetise Pinterest with "promoted pins", which actually meant, it was now open to putting up advertisements.

The photo bookmarking site now has more than 100 million monthly users. Pinterest is where users save and share their image collections of a whole lot of things online—

such collections range in theme from recipes and hairstyles to crafts and home décor. In May 2015 it was valued at $11 billion, placing co-founders, Silbermann and Evan Sharp, definitively into the ranks of billionaires.

Despite all the success and that too when he is yet to reach 35, Silbermann though remains the soft spoken, thoughtful individual that he was as a young man from Des Moines. He is still reluctant about giving too many interviews, though when he speaks, his words ooze intelligence. He is married to an Indian-origin woman, Divya Bhaskaran and the couple have a son named Max. Silbermann's success has garnered him a great deal of media attention from around the world. In 2014, he topped the *Fortune* magazine's list of "Top 40 Under 40", young entrepreneurs while the next year; he ranked at number 15 on *Forbes* List of America's Richest Entrepreneurs Under 40.

REFERENCE

1. https://www.theguardian.com/technology/2014/apr/05/pinterest-interview-ben-silbermann-social-media

□

5
Bill Gates

Software mogul and co-founder of Microsoft, Bill Gates is the richest man in US and the second-richest in the world. As on July 2016, the self-made billionaire currently enjoys a net worth of $76.8 billion and that too after giving away $28 billion to charitable causes. Despite Gates moving away from day-to-day running of Microsoft, its shares continue to soar and his investment vehicle Cascade keeps raking in the profits.

Early Life

Born as William Henry Gates III on October 28, 1955, in Seattle, Washington, the future software billionaire grew up in the heart of a typically upper middle-class American family with two siblings, elder sister Kristianne and a younger sister Libby. Aware of their son's immense potential, the Gates enrolled thirteen year old Bill at Seattle's exclusive preparatory Lakeside School. He did well in almost all his subjects and was especially brilliant in math and science. However it was computers which hooked him when a Seattle computer company introduced students of Lakeside to this invention. It was here that young Bill met Paul Allen and forged a friendship over a common passion for computers that would later translate into a thriving business partnership.

Gates graduated from high school in 1973. With him scoring an incredible 1590 out of 1600 in the college SAT test, his parents hoped that he would sail through any college course that he chose. Though Gates enrolled in the Harvard University to study for a degree in law, he ended up spending more time in the computer lab than in classes. During this time, Gates and Allen teamed up to write a software program for a New Mexico based company that had just launched a mini-computer named Altair. While Allen had already dropped out of Washington State University, the acceptance of their software program by MITS in New Mexico prompted Gates to quit college too, much to the dismay of his parents.

Birth of Microsoft

In 1975, Gates and Allen formally cemented their partnership by launching a company named 'Microsoft', which was a fusion of "Micro-computer" and "Software". The hyphen was soon dropped from the name and the company started writing BASIC software program for the Altair computer. However Gates was not totally satisfied working for MITS and would often get into arguments with the management. Besides he was also unhappy with the practice of free distribution and use of software that his company had created.

In 1980, IBM, one of the largest technology companies of the time, asked Microsoft to write software to run their new personal computer, the IBM PC. Gates was astute enough to demand that Microsoft would retain the licensing rights for the operating system, MS-DOS. This enabled Microsoft to earn money for every computer sold first by IBM, and later by all the other companies that made PC computers.

Microsoft grew quickly from 25 employees in 1978 to over 128 in 1981. During this time, Microsoft's Revenue too exploded from $2.5 million to $16 million. In mid-1981 Gates and Allen incorporated Microsoft, after which Gates was appointed President and Chairman of the Board while Allen was named Executive Vice President.

The next milestone in the growth of Microsoft came when in 1985 it launched 'Windows' which replaced the text-and-keyboard driven MS-DOS with graphic user interface driven by a mouse. This made it easier for the non-technical users who were not so fluent with coding and instead would prefer a simpler display of text and images on the screen that could be operated by a mouse. All these innovations led to a phenomenal growth of the company.

In March 1986, Microsoft went public with an initial public offering (IPO) of $21 per share. At the time Gates owned 45 per cent of the company's 24.7 million shares which made him an overnight millionaire at the age of only 31. Out of $520 million shares, Gates owned $234 million shares of the Microsoft. Over time, the company's stock continued to spiral upward. In 1987 Gates became a billionaire when the stock raised to $90.75 a share while in 1999, when stock prices touched an all time high, Gates' net worth touched a staggering $101 billion.

Over the years, Microsoft went on to develop many new technologies and some of the world's most popular software and products such as Word and PowerPoint as well as web browsers like Internet Explorer and Edge. In recent years it has gone in for several high-profile acquisitions like its 2011 takeover of Skype Technologies for $8.5 billion as well as its June 2016 deal of buying LinkedIn for $26.2 billion. With an employee base of more than a hundred thousand and a presence in practically every country of the world, Microsoft's vision of "A computer on every desk and Microsoft software on every computer", seems close to reality.

Life beyond Microsoft

Gates owns roughly 2.5 per cent of Microsoft, which accounts for slightly less than 15 per cent of his fortune. Most of his wealth comes from investments managed by the reputed asset management firm, Cascade Investment LLC.

This Kirkland-based firm is headed by Michael Larson who is the main person responsible for investing Gates' personal wealth in companies like Canadian National Railway, agricultural machinery manufacturer Deere & Co., waste collection outfit Republic Services, the drinks group Femsa as well as hygiene and water technology firm Ecolab. In October 2015, Gates also invested in Impossible Foods, a startup that has plans of creating plant-based foods with the natural taste of meat but that would use fewer resources to produce.

Bill Gates chose as his life partner Melinda French of Dallas who once worked as a Microsoft Manager. The two got married on New Year's Day in 1994 on the Hawaiian island of Lanai. Today the couple has three children and they live in Medina, Washington. Both Bill and Melinda Gates are actively involved in philanthropy with charitable and scientific research constituting their main areas of support. During his leisure, Bill Gates enjoys reading, playing golf, bridge and tennis.

In recent times, Gates has been deeply committed to philanthropic initiatives. In 1994, with his wife, he founded the Bill & Melinda Gates Foundation that is worth around $40 billion. Gates himself contributed $28 billion to the Foundation which is not surprisingly today the largest transparently operated private foundation in the world. The foundation is primarily committed to the promotion of healthcare and reduction of extreme poverty in the world and expansion of educational opportunities and access to Information Technology (IT) in America. Among its most successful projects has been the use of vaccines and healthcare initiatives in developing countries.

In December 2015, at the United Nations climate talks in Paris, Gates unveiled the Breakthrough Energy Coalition which brings together more than 20 billionaires, committed to investing in innovative clean energy. The Coalition has roped in the business leaders like Facebook co-founder Mark

Zuckerberg, Chinese e-commerce billionaire Jack Ma, and Africa's richest man Aliko Dangote. According to him, "Our primary goal with the coalition is as much to accelerate progress on clean energy as it is to make a profit".

□

6
Binny and Sachin Bansal

Though not related to each other, Binny and Sachin Bansal together can be credited with pioneering e-commerce in the Indian market. Friends from their IIT days, Binny Bansal and Sachin Bansal are the co-founders of 'Flipkart', the first originally Indian online store that started with selling books and then expanded to include a whole range of electronics, gadgets and lifestyle products. With the acquisition of the popular online apparel store, Myntra.com, Flipkart is now a major player in the Indian e-commerce scene and in May 2015, enjoyed a net worth of US $15.5 billion US, according to *Forbes*. This makes Binny and Sachin Bansal not only among the richest digital entrepreneurs in the country, with a net worth of US $1.16 billion each but an inspiration to thousands of young Indians who dream of having successful startups.

Early Life

Despite being unrelated to each other, Sachin and Binny Bansal were actually brought up in the same city, Chandigarh and incredibly, studied the same school though at the time they were not very familiar to one another. However certain biographical differences make any study of their journeys interesting.

Sachin Bansal was born on 5 August 1981 in Chandigarh (UT). His father was a businessman and his mother, a homemaker. Being a brilliant student through his school life, it did not come as much of a surprise when Sachin got through the premier Indian Institute of Technology (IIT). He joined IIT, Delhi and graduated with a degree in computer science. Despite an early fascination with gaming, he took up a job with Techspan right after leaving college.

In January 2006 came an important change in Sachin's career graph when he joined Amazon.com as a Senior Software Engineer. Amazon was at the time already a global e-commerce giant and thus this proved to be the ideal place to learn about the e-commerce business. Sachin soon realized that India was ready to welcome a home-grown online retailer and with the aim of doing something similar, he also convinced Binny Bansal to join Amazon.

Like Sachin, Binny too grew up in Chandigarh but was different from his future partner in being a bookworm as a child—apparently Salman Rushdie eventually became one of his most favourite writers. At the same time Binny was also an avid sportsman and reportedly served as the captain of the Basketball team of his school and college. Again, at one time he used to be a great fan of Chicago Bulls. Binny's father was employed in the banking sector while his mother was in government service.

Binny first came in touch with Sachin at IIT, Delhi where he enrolled in computer engineering degree programme. After graduation, Binny went to work with Sarnoff Corporation. Here he proved his engineering genius, developing a lane sensor device for cars which would alert drivers changing lanes without giving a signal with a warning beep. This safety feature proved to be very popular and made him a success in his company. As convinced by Sachin he left Sarnoff after one and half year to join Amazon where both recognized the absence of home-grown online retailers in the Indian market. This was a crucial time of learning the ropes as both would go on to found a company that would go on to usher in the wave of online shopping in the country.

The Birth of Flipkart

Sachin and Binny Bansal took the plunge in October 2007 when they left Amazon and coughed up Rs. 2 lakh each to launch their own e-commerce site. This was named 'Flipkart' and at first the idea was to sell only books. This was aided by two computers rigged up in their two-bedroom apartment in Koramangala, mainly a residential locality in Bangalore. For the first ten days, there was not even a single sale on the site. But then the tide turned and the site received its first order from a customer located in Andhra Pradesh for the book titled, 'Leaving Microsoft to Change the World', by John Wood. According to an interesting anecdote, Binny Bansal who was in charge of logistics, did not even have enough cash on him and had to borrow money from a friend to buy the copy of the book to ship it to the first Flipkart customer. Even then, the site continued to struggle initially and the monthly allowance of Rs. 10,000 that the founders got from their parents for almost 18 months helped to keep the startup afloat.

Success at Last

In the next five years, as the online bookstore expanded to sell everything from electronics and gadgets to apparel and personal care products, the founders had to raise about US$ 190 million (over Rs. 1,150 crore), mainly from Tiger Global and Accel Partners. High expenses eventually put the site in danger of becoming an unviable business after which the Bansals were compelled to tighten the belt at Flipkart. Among the measures taken were re-organizing the employee structure, using more of technology and closing down the music download section which failed to be a hit with customers. At the same time, the site began moving away from being a direct seller of products to partnering up with other retailers who were interested in using the Flipkart credibility to attract customers.

In 2013, came another massive cash infusion-around $360 million (about Rs. 2,200 crore) in two tranches, with South African Internet Giant Naspers, Russian billionaire Yuri Milner's DST Global and Qatar Investment Authority being the main investors. In 2014, Flipkart reached an important milestone—its $1-billion (Rs. 6,100 crore) sales mark—and with that its reputation as the first Indian e-commerce success story was cemented. In 2015, there were reports in media of another round of funding—about $500 million—with Tiger Global believed to be the main investor. This reportedly put the valuation of Flipkart at $15.5 billion and made the founder duo worth around $1.6 billion each, thanks to identical stakes of 7.5 per cent each in the company.

Headquartered in Bangalore, Flipkart today has an employee strength of 33,000—it has a listing of more than 30 million products and has 45 million registered users. The site ships 8 million packages a month and serves more than a thousand cities and towns in the country. This success propelled Sachin Bansal and Binny Bansal in the *Forbes* India Rich List for the first time in September 2015, at the 86th position with a net worth of US$ 1.3 billion each, thus making them the first entrepreneurs from Indian e-commerce entrepreneurs to emerge as billionaires.

□

7

Brian Acton and Jan Koum

With Whatsapp now being used as a verb in contemporary usage, it is evident just how popular this online messaging app has become the world over. And the genius behind its creation was a team of computer programmers, namely Brian Acton and Jan Koum. With the app being acquired by Facebook in 2014 for a staggering sum of 22 billion USD in cash and stocks, Acton walked away a billionaire. In June 2016, he enjoys a net worth of 4.6 billion USD and figures on *Forbes* 2016 list of the top 400 billionaires of the world.

Early Life

Brian Acton was born on February 24, 1972 in Michigan but as his family moved to Central Florida, he grew up in the balmy environs of the sunshine state. His mother was an entrepreneur herself and used to run a successful freight-shipping firm which in turn gave young Acton valuable insight into running a business and meeting payroll. After graduating from Lake Howell High School, he enrolled in Stanford University where he earned a degree in computer science in 1994. By that time he was already working as a systems administrator for Rockwell International after which he went on to become a product tester at Apple Inc. and

Adobe Systems. Acton was among the earliest employees at Yahoo Inc when he joined the company in 1996.

Unlike Acton, Jan Koum saw tough days in early childhood. He was born in Kyiv, Ukraine on February 24, 1976. He arrived in the US when his mother and grandmother immigrated to Mountain View, California in 1992. Initially the family had to take recourse to a social support program to get a small two-bedroom apartment. During this time Koum's mother worked as a babysitter, while Koum himself contributed to family expenses by working as cleaner at a grocery. However his innate genius for computers was evident by the time he turned 18. He joined the San Jose State University even as he was working for Ernst and Young as a security tester.

Budding Entrepreneur

While working at Yahoo, Acton met infrastructure engineer, Jan Koum who too had joined the company in 1998. Though they continued to work at Yahoo, at the same time the duo kept exploring ideas on innovations in the digital world. However Acton's initial ventures were not successful and had suffered major losses when the dot com bubble burst in the early 2000s. In 2007, jaded by the monotony of their work, both Koum and Acton left Yahoo to embark on a year-long sabbatical through South America. Upon their return, they applied for work in Facebook but were rejected.

It was around this time that Koum bought an i-Phone and discovered the wonders of its App Store. Convinced that smartphone apps were going to be the next big thing, Koum set about developing a messaging app. He chose the name Whatsapp as it sounded close to the common greeting "What's up", and on February 24, 2009—which also happened to be his birthday—Whatsapp was incorporated as a company in California.

However, the earliest versions of Whatsapp encountered several problems like crashing and failure to update—so much so that Koum was on the verge of giving it up. At this point Acton pitched in with valuable support and encouraged Koum to give the app few more months. When the latter developed Whatsapp 2.0 with a messaging component, it struck a chord with the users and its popularity soared to 250,000.

Acton on his part convinced five of their former Yahoo co-workers to cough up 250,000 USD in seed funding and in return, obtain a co-founder status as well as a healthy stake in the company. On November 1, 2009, Acton formally joined Whatsapp Inc and set about attracting more investments.

Whatsapp was first launched in November 2009 on the App Store for the iPhone, following which, a version for the Blackberry was also developed. With the release of its Android version in August 2010, Whatsapp was set to dominate the world. This soon came to be true as according to Koum's own admission through Twitter in August 2014, Whatsapp had over 600 million active users worldwide. By next year, Whatsapp was the most globally popular messaging app, with more than 600 million active users till January 2015 which had ballooned to one billion in a little more than a year, as of February 2016. Interestingly India accounted for the largest number of users with 65 million active users, making up around 10 per cent of the global user base of Whatsapp.

In 2014, after rounds of hectic negotiation between Facebook and Whatsapp, the former acquired the messaging app for $22 billion USD in cash and stock, according to Forbes.com. The deal resulted in Acton getting richer by 3 billion USD in stock and cash for his stake in Whatsapp. In all, life seemed to have to a full circle as five years before the same company that had rejected Acton's application for employment now toed his terms of acquisition. At the time the deal became famous as not only Facebook's most expensive acquisition but also as the largest purchase of a venture-backed company in history.

Continuing Innovations

Only three days after the acquisition of Whatsapp by Facebook, Koum announced the launch of its voice-calling service. Another new initiative would be the sale of new smartphones under the Whatsapp brand in Germany—this was in keeping with the founders' ambitious vision of the presence of Whatsapp in all smartphones on the planet.

To a large extent the success of Whatsapp has been due to the steadfast effort of the co-founders to keep it free from advertising and other trivia. In fact, Koum still has a note taped to his desk that he got Acton to write and sign, promising "No ads! No games! No gimmicks!" This is indicative of the strong commitment of its creators to keep Whatsapp a genuine communications service and nothing more.

□

8

Brian Chesky

Getting a good place to stay comprises among the top worries of travellers in peak season—whether those on a holiday or business tour. What if travellers could book rooms and houses belonging to other people in the place they are visiting and that too with the ease of the internet? This is just what Brian Chesky thought when he started 'Airbnb', the online home rental service that has become one of the most popular lodging options for travellers in the world today. The success of the Airbnb company in turn has rocketed Chesky to the list of top contemporary internet entrepreneurs and as of June 2016, has blessed him with a present net worth of 3.3 billion USD, according to *Forbes*.

Early Life

Brian Chesky born on August 29, 1981 to Deborah and Robert H. Chesky, who were both social workers. He grew up in Niskayuna, New York with his younger sister Allison. Right from his childhood, he displayed a lively interest in art and design—his leisure hours would be spent in drawing and painting as well as designing shoes, toys and gadgets. This early interest gradually evolved into a passion for landscape art during his adult years. In 1999, after graduating from high school, Brian joined the prestigious Rhode Island School of Design. There he pursued a bachelor's degree in industrial design and in 2004, graduated from the college. In those days such was his passion for art that he was rarely seen without a sketchbook and a pen. It was also in the college that he met Joe Gebbia—with whom he would later enter into a successful business partnership.

Budding Entrepreneur

However even before he had earned his degree, Chesky gave evidence of his natural entrepreneurial skills. In college, he and his friends managed a hockey team named NADS. At one time, the team faced the threat of derecognize upon which Chesky with his mates, took on the challenge to transform it into a brand. One of the consequences of this re-branding effort was the creation of Scrotie, a highly popular mascot, that eventually came to be identified with the team of the college itself. Not only Brian's team was saved from being disqualified, but he recognized his knack for entrepreneurship within himself.

Starting Own Venture

After graduating from college, Chesky took up a job at 3DID, Inc in Los Angeles as an industrial designer and strategist. Later however he moved to San Francisco, where he took up an apartment with Gebbia, his mate from college.

In 2007, during a conference, organized by the Industrial Designers Society of America in San Francisco, Chesky noted the desperation of visitors who could not find a place to stay in the city. With all hotel rooms were booked, participants of the conference were having trouble finding accommodation. On the other hand, Chesky and Gebbia were at a tight spot in their finances as their rent was due. Chesky recognized the potential of the situation and saw how both sides could benefit. He promptly bought three air mattresses and marketed the "Airbed and Breakfast", at his place—an initiative that was lapped up three attendees to the city conference who stayed in his apartment. The guests were relieved to find a place to stay while Chesky and Gebbia had earned some cash in the process.

This experience provided the germ of the idea which Chesky developed into 'Airbedandbreakfast.com' in February 2008 after roping in Harvard graduate and technical architect Nathan Blecharczyk who became the third co-founder of the company. Chesky took on the role of CEO and started looking for investors. As part of their funding effort, the founders even came up with the idea of special-edition, cereals titled "Obama O's" and "Cap'n McCains", based on then Presidential candidates Barack Obama and John McCain. The innovative cereal boxes caught the attention of Y Combinator who agreed to invest in Chesky's startup.

In the very first year of its existence, Airbnb began expanding in Europe. But with expansion, came certain problems like tenant vandalism. In response to such issues, Chesky added important features in the Airbnb service like a guarantee for theft or vandalism, more staff support as well as a round-the-clock helpline. These measures played an important role in raising the popularity of Airbnb and during the 2014 FIFA World Cup, hosted in Brazil, around 120,000 people opted to stay at Airbnb homes.

Brian Chesky has claimed that a major reason for the success of Airbnb goes to the company's policy of enhancing the service. He believes that both the guest and the host should have a pleasant travel experience and only then the network will expand and grow. To bring this about, Chesky insists on collecting feedback from customers—indeed at one time in the early stages of the company, he and his employees were actually out on the streets, asking people what they would like in such an online room rental service, what would comprise of their concerns and what would make them opt for the same service provider again. In this way, collecting insights from potential and actual customers, their suggestions as well as complaints and then working upon them has gone a long way in shaping the Airbnb into a successful company that it is today. According to *Forbes*, the service operates in 34,000 cities in 190 countries and till February 2016, more than 60 million guests have used the rental service.

Chesky himself has shot into fame with his highly popular startup and is now counted among the most successful of contemporary tech entrepreneurs. He owns around a 13 per cent stake in the company. Chesky was ranked 7th in *Forbes* 2015 list of Richest Entrepreneurs under 2015. The same year in May the Obama Administration named Chesky a Presidential Ambassador for Global Entrepreneurship.

□

9
Chad Hurley

In this age of online entertainment, which isn't hooked on to YouTube where one can search for videos, post and share them with viewers around the world! This is what Chad Hurley is famous for, who with Steve Chen and Jawed Karim, co-founded the site and then went on to become one of the biggest success stories of the digital world.

Early Life

Born as Chad Meredith Hurley on January 24, 1977 in Reading, Pennsylvania, the future internet sensation was the third child of Don and Joann Hurley. Chad grew up with an older sister and brother and proved his mettle practically in every sphere of activity. Right from elementary school, he gave evidence of his passion for arts—he not only made sketches and paintings but also sold them from a makeshift shop on the sidewalk outside his home—thus giving early evidence of a strong entrepreneurial streak that would later make him an internet success.

At the same time, Hurley was a keen student of computers and electronic media. While attending Twin Valley High School, he was also a member of Technology Student Association. Again this interest would eventually lead him in the direction of internet and his achievements in the online world.

Incredibly Hurley was also a standout runner for his age and was primarily responsible for taking his school's cross country program to two state-level titles in 1992 and 1994.

After completing high school in 1995, Hurley enrolled into the Indiana University of Pennsylvania from where he graduated with a Bachelors' of Arts degree in 1999, majoring in his long-time passion, Fine Arts.

Stint at PayPal

After college, Hurley's first major job was at the online payment processing site PayPal. He had read about the company in *Wired* magazine and soon dashed off an e-mail to them, asking if they had any vacancies. When called for an interview, Chad impressed the management by creating a logo for the company, then and there. Not surprisingly, he was hired on the spot in the role of the official graphic designer.

A major fallout of Hurley's stint at PayPal was his friendship with another employee, Steve Chen who would go on to become his future business partner. The two friends remained at PayPal till eBay's acquisition in 2002 after which Hurley left to work as a consultant in the Silicon Valley. Chen however stayed back at PayPal for another two years, during which he supervised the entry of the company in the Chinese market.

Success with YouTube

In 2005 the two friends came together again to found YouTube, a video-sharing website which would change the face of online entertainment. The story of its birth goes back to January that year. Chen hosted a get-together for his friends at his home and invited Hurley as well. The party was recorded on a camcorder and digital camera, but emailing the clips to other guests proved difficult because of the big file size. This set Hurley and Chen thinking about how to send videos to contacts, and then they came up with the idea of a website where a user could upload and share videos with the rest of the world. In this they took some inspiration from Flickr, a photo-sharing site that had just been launched and turned out to be exceedingly popular among netizens. Hurley and Chen spotted a similar need for sharing videos online and this is how YouTube was launched in 2005.

During the initial stages of the development of the site, Hurley and Chen had just around them people working for them and that too without any pay for most of the time. Hurley took on the job of the tagging and video-sharing aspects of YouTube. Soon the site started getting noticed and within just a year of its launch, became the tenth most popular site in the world.

Indeed such was the success of YouTube that search giant Google approached Hurley and Chen with a proposal for acquisition. In 2006, Google Inc took over YouTube for a whopping $1.65 billion. Based on Google's registration statement with SEC filed on February 7, 2007, the *Wall Street Journal* reported that Chad Hurley's share in the deal was $345.6 million at Google's February 7, 2007 closing stock price of $470.01. Hurley in fact received $694,087 in Google shares directly and another $41,232 shares in a trust. Even after the acquisition, Hurley continued as the CEO of YouTube till 2010 whereupon he remained as an advisor for the company.

Other Ventures

After YouTube, Hurley and Chen came together again to found a new company called AVOS. And in 2011 AVOS acquired the Yahoo-owned bookmarking service, Delicious. Both Hurley and Chen struck this deal with the aim of creating new ideas within an already existing program and seeing if it could be turned into a successful enterprise.

Two years later Hurley and his business partner launched another company called 'MixBit' which offers video editing services on smartphones. Hurley is currently the CEO of MixBit.

Interests Outside Computers

Despite the success that Hurley earned in his Internet businesses, he always dreamed of following his first passion, Art. And with this in mind, he co-founded with Anthony Mazzei, his own clothing brand in 1994, titled 'Hlaska'. This brand invokes the fusion of the names of two states—Hawaii and Alaska. When this venture of Hurley's raised a few eyebrows in the tech media, he explained by saying that he did not find any major differences between the two spheres of activity—while the brand creates apparel that the designers would want to wear themselves, the bags and wallets designed here are something that they would want to buy. As was with YouTube, Hurley created a product to fulfil an existing need and something that would be good enough for him to use himself.

Hurley's interest in sports has also found expression through investments. He is a part-owner of the Golden State Warriors team in the NBA and the Major Soccer League's Los Angeles Football Club. He was also a major investor with US F1 Team, that was slated to make its debut in 'Formula One', automobile racing for the 2010 season. However on March 2, 2010, the team was unofficially shut down and its staff relieved of their duties. The reason for this was never disclosed but Hurley remains optimistic about the team getting together again.

Chad Hurley is married to Kathy Clark, daughter of successful Silicon Valley entrepreneur, Jim Clark. The Hurleys have two children.

Today Hurley serves as an inspiration to other startups as a beacon of success. Thanks to the stock options that he received from Google during the acquisition of YouTube, Hurley is a billionaire. The same year, in 2006, Hurley was ranked No. 28 on *Business 2.0* magazine's "50 People Who Matter" list.

Apart from being a financial success, Hurley has proved to be a star innovator. YouTube has been hailed as one of the most popular services on the internet where at least 100 million clips are viewed daily and an additional 65,000 new videos are uploaded every 24 hours. Though initially the site was ridiculed as having an appeal only for amateurs who would use it for uploading their cat and dog videos, eventually it proved to be much more. YouTube now boasts of an extensive and varied archive of inspiration and instructional videos besides emerging as an online community where users can share news of their part of the world and voice their opinions.

□

10

Christopher Poole

Christopher Poole is an American digital entrepreneur who has explored many possibilities of the anonymity of the internet through his startups. He is best known as the founder of '4chan', an internet message board that he administered through a secret online identity known as 'moot'. After the huge popularity of 4chan, Poole was prompted to launch yet another website known as 'Canvas' where users can upload digitally altered photos. In March 2016 Poole was reported to have joined Google, though his role in the company was not disclosed.

Early Life

Christopher Poole was born in the year 1988. While still in high school, Poole started a message board in 2003 and on this he adopted a secret persona, named 'moot'. At the time he was just fifteen years old but the precocious teen's creation turned out to be exceedingly popular with the younger generation of internet users.

Budding Developer

When asked in an interview as to the choice of his pseudonym, Poole revealed that it goes back to an online moniker, "moo" that he often used as a teenager. The origin of 4chan is equally interesting—apparently during a summer break, Poole was while surfing the internet, got hooked to Japanese animation and particularly the anime on online forums. This was further heightened with his discovery of an image-board Web forum named 2chan. Since the code for this site was publicly available, Poole used online tools to translate it from Japanese to English. To honour his inspiration, he wanted to adopt a similar name for his site, but as the URL for 3chan was already taken then, he settled for the next available number—and this is how 4chan got its name.

The 4chan is a group of message boards where users can post almost anything-ranging from pictures of pretty puppies to sometimes disturbing images and language too. Among these /b/ is the designated "random" board of 4chan where almost all posts are sent anonymously. In fact, /b/ can be read as a reverse panopticon, in this sense—nobody can view anybody on the site while everybody can claim to speak from the centre. A post here usually consists of an image and a few lines of text. Other message boards on 4chan cater to interests varying from like travel and photography to adult content even.

Not surprisingly, 4chan has a brush with the law now and then. Apart from the presence of adult content, users often play pranks which result in the cops calling in. For example in late 2006 someone posted a bomb threat on the site while a user was accused of hacking the then Governor of Alaska Sarah Palin's e-mail account and posting it on 4chan before it ended up on Gawker. In response to these incidents, 4chan has attempted to clean up its message boards by having moderators delete abusive material as well as calls to disrupt other sites.

Poole himself has admitted that users on 4chan often post abusive language—however he points out that just because 4chan is hosting it, does not mean that he agree with it. He is clear about the difference between him personally opposing such abusive language and content while at the same time supporting the freedom which allows a site like this to exist.

4chan today has millions of users and its network of message boards draw more than 200 million page views a month. According to Poole himself, it is the largest active forum in the United States with 8.2 million unique visitors every month and 600 million page loads per month. On an average, visitors remain on the site for about 19 minutes at a time and view 30 pages each. Additionally the site gets around 800,000 new posts a day. Indeed many of the strange memes floating about on the Internet, including LOLcats, can be traced back to 4chan—such has been its impact on mainstream culture.

Newer Directions

In 2010, Poole announced a new online venture titled 'Canvas' after he reportedly raised a sum of $625,000. The website went live on January 31, 2011. On this, users could upload digitally modified images—however users needed to identify themselves by using Facebook Connect. In January 2014, Poole however broke the news that Canvas together with its DrawQuest feature, would be closing down.

Almost exactly a year later, in January 2015, Poole announced that he would be stepping down as the 4chan administrator and on 23rd of the same month, he hosted his last Question and Answer Session with site users in his online persona of 'moot'. This retirement kick-started the process of handing over the site to three anonymous moderators even as Poole began looking for a buyer for the site. On September 21, 2015, it was reported in the tech media2 that 4chan would be acquired by Hiroyuki Nishimura, founder of the Japanese BBS 2channel. Eventually on March 7, 2016, Poole admitted that he too had moved on and accepted a position with the search engine giant, Google.

Poole and Internet Anonymity

Poole has often come under criticism for creating a web forum like 4chan where users can post anonymously and which consequently often results in offensive or abusive content on the site. However he has remained a strong advocate for internet anonymity, saying that this allows people to forgive, forget and in a way, move on. Poole remains opposed to what he calls, "A state of persistent identity", that is taking place on Facebook and many other social networking sites. According to him this is a dangerous trend as it in ten years' time, everything one says or does will be visible online and forever be linked to a user's real identity.

REFERENCES

1. http://bits.blogs.nytimes.com/2010/03/19/one-on-one-christopher-poole-founder-of-4chan/?_r=0
2. http://bits.blogs.nytimes.com/2015/09/21/4chan-sells-to-japanese-web-culture-pioneer-2channel/?_r=0

□

11
Craig Newmark

Anyone in the English-speaking world who has ever thought of putting up a classifieds of any sort, is more likely than not to have thought of craigslist.com. This is one of the top ten most-visited web portals in English and is the brainchild of American internet entrepreneur, Craig Newmark. His online classifieds site has made him one of the most successful internet entrepreneurs with a net worth of 400 million USD, as of 2010, as well as a listing in 2010 *Forbes* "15 Billionaires In The Making".

Early Life

Craig Newmark was born on December 6, 1952 in Morristown, New Jersey of United States. His father Lee Newmark was an insurance salesman, who unfortunately died when Craig was just thirteen. His mother Joyce Newmark was then compelled to move to an apartment with Craig and his brother Jeff. Though his childhood was marked by financial difficulties, Craig was an intelligent student and after passing from Morristown High School in 1971, he managed to bag scholarships, which helped him to earn a Bachelor of Science degree in 1975 from Case Western Reserve University. Two years later he graduated with Master of Science degree from the same university during which he wrote a thesis on, "Fundamental Models of

Computer Systems and Their Relationship to Information Security."

After college, Newmark took up a job as a programmer with IBM where he worked for seventeen long years—all this while he moved across various places like New Jersey, Boca Raton in Florida and Detroit.

Success with Craigslist

Year 1993 proved to be a momentous one for Newmark as he decided to take up a job with Charles Schwab and moved to San Francisco. This was the right time and place to be for those hooked to the immense possibilities offered by the internet.

As Newmark browsed through the medium, he discovered the lack of a free but really exhaustive classifieds site. In 1995 thus he launched 'craigslist'—originally this was more of an online forum where people would post information about events and opportunities in San Francisco without any charge. Over time, it became a highly popular site for posting advertisements, especially related to jobs and housing, and then personals too. While most of the listings are still free, its job postings in 18 cities as well as brokered apartments in New York does attract a fee. However in recent years its section on adult content ads garnered a lot of negative feedback and was forced to shut down in 2010. On the whole though the site, the popularity of craigslist remains undisputed. The portal exists in 70 countries and gets more than 20 billion page views per month. According to *Forbes*, if the site cleaned up its listings, allowed ads and charged for postings in all cities, it could be worth more than 3 billion USD.

Even after twenty years of craigslist's existence, Newmark remains involved with the operation of the online portal; he continues to work with craigslist as a customer service representative as well as in the capacity of neutralizing scamming and spamming.

Other Ventures

In March 2011 Newmark started 'craigconnects', whose aim is to publicize philanthropic initiatives being taken around the world, thereby inspiring others to give back to society as well. Another aspect of craigconnects is the promotion of media integrity. Apart from this, Newmark is part of the board of directors of three non-profit organizations as well as on the advisory board of eleven others. In all these, Newmark's intention is to support initiatives that range from veteran welfare and funding for school projects to those which assist government or social schemes with the use of internet technology. In 2006 Newmark also contributed 10,000 USD towards the efforts of New Assignment. Net, a non-profit group that brings together professionals and amateurs with the aim of producing investigative stories on the Internet.

Personal Life

Craig Newmark is married to Eileen Whelpley since December 2012 and the couple lives in Cole Valley, in San Francisco. Even though he attended a Jewish religious school in childhood, Newmark now describes himself as a non-practicing, secular Jew, adding in a lighter vein that he considers singer Leonard Cohen his rabbi. Despite the controversies that craigslist has sometimes brought Newmark's way, his success remains undoubted—his inclusion in *Forbes'* 2010 List of Billionaires in the Making is only one evidence of this fact.

□

12
Daniel Ek

For people fond of western music and keen to have legal access to it on the internet, 'Spotify' is not an unfamiliar name. It is one of the most popular legal music streaming services online and was co-founded by Swedish tech expert and entrepreneur—Daniel Ek.

Early Life

Daniel Ek was born on February 21, 1983 in the Swedish capital city of Stockholm. He was raised in Ragsved, near Stockholm, and since the early days music and computers were the two main interests in his life. This is hardly surprising considering he had an opera singer and a jazz pianist for his maternal grandparents. Though Ek's father had left the family when he was still a baby, he had been raised by his stepfather who worked in the IT industry and hence encouraged an interest in computers in the little boy. Eventually Ek became an expert at computers, internet and coding. The entrepreneurial bug bit him early and when still in his teens, he was building websites for firms as well as running Web hosting services. At the age of 16, obsessed with Google's speed, he applied to be an engineer there and then set out to build his own search company.

After high school Ek enrolled in Sweden's Royal Institute of Technology to study engineering. However the focus on theoretical mathematics during the first year of the course bored him and he decided to quit to follow his passion for internet ventures. After working for a series of online companies, Ek founded his first major business, 'Advertigo', which offered online marketing services. This soon became a success and caught the attention of Swedish company, Tradedoubler which acquired it for 1 million USD in 2006. Ek made an additional 1 million USD by selling patents related to Advertigo.

Thus at 23, Ek was already a self-made millionaire. Determined to live the fast life, he blew up his money on a swanky three-bedroom apartment in central Stockholm, a bright red Ferrari Modena as well as hip socializing. However soon he faced a burnout and realized the essential hollowness of this kind of life. Instead he retreated to a log cabin in the mountains and took some time off to take stock of what he wanted to do with his life. Only the thought of music gave him comfort and Ek started thinking how he could combine it with his other interest, internet technology.

Success with Spotify

Ek's deal with Tradedoubler had resulted in another important consequence—it had brought him in contact with company's co-founder, Martin Lorentzon. Ek's ideas on founding a legal online music streaming found adequate support in Lorentzon and the two then co-founded a company named 'Spotify AB' in Stockholm.

There is an interesting anecdote related to the naming of the company. Apparently Ek and Lorentzon were sitting in two different rooms at the former's apartment, yelling out possible titles for a music site, when one of Lorentzon's suggestions was misinterpreted by Ek as 'Spotify' but which eventually stuck. However the website took longer to develop and eventually in October 2008, the company launched its legal music streaming service 'Spotify'.

At the time, there were just two major options for music fans who wished to listen to it online—either download it illegally from sites like Napster or buy an expensive service like from Apple's iTunes store. This not only restricted options for music lovers but proved harmful for the music industry too. For instance while recording industry revenue was a substantial 56.7 billion USD in 1999, by 2011 it had plummeted to just about 30 billion USD.

In came Ek with a refreshingly different business model that came to be nicknamed 'freemium'. With Spotify, he offered a legal music streaming service that was free for the basic version but would attract a subscription for premium versions which would provide additional features. The free version would be supported for occasional advertisements.

This model quickly proved to be popular. By January 2012 Spotify had racked up 10 million active users who could claim to have access to 15 million songs on their computers, just for the cost of hearing a commercial now and then.

Another important aspect of Spotify was its integrating it with social media. Ek entered into a deal with Facebook to embed it into Spotify's platform and vice versa. This enabled users to share playlists with contacts—in fact more than 1.5 billion songs have been exchanged on Facebook so far. With this business model, Spotify has not only been able to stem piracy but offer a healthy boost to the global music industry too.

Not surprisingly, all this success helped Spotify attract ample funding. Though it started out with small-time Swedish sponsors, eventually it garnered funding from major social media names like Li Ka-shing, Sean Parker and FoundersFund. In all this amounted to more than 50 million USD and took up the company's valuation to roughly 250 million USD. In the summer of 2011, Spotify further attracted a 100 million USD funding from DST, Accel and Kleiner Perkins, taking up its valuation to 1 billion USD.

By early 2012, Spotify boasted of 2.5 million paying customers worldwide, of which 85 per cent were subscribers of the monthly 10 USD portability charge while the rest were subscribers of the ad-free feature. With this and its advertising revenue, Spotify was estimated to generate revenues of around 300 million USD. According to analysts, if Pandora could be used as a comp, that would make Spotify worth more than 2 billion USD and its co-founder Ek, worth over $300 million, at least on paper.

Daniel Ek continues to be the CEO and on the lookout for developing newer features at Spotify to attract users. He still holds about 15 per cent of the company while the other co-founder Lorentzon owns some 20 per cent. Eventually Ek wishes to nurture Spotify into something bigger than a music player that allows legal access to almost every song on the planet, on demand, for free. With Spotify, his vision is to create an alternate business model for music where the recording industry and such music streaming services will exist in synergetic harmony.

□

13
Dennis Crowley

Social networking apps are all the rage in these times of instant communication and media-driven self-worth. While some like Facebook dominate the market by the sheer number of their users, others like Foursquare appeal with their special features. And the brain behind Foursquare is that of Dennis Crowley who co-founded the location-driven social networking app with Naveen Selvadurai in 2008. Eventually Foursquare turned out to be a highly popular mobile app with a registered user base of 45 million, as of December 2013. This gave Crowley an approximate net worth of 30 million USD, as of late 2012. He was the CEO of the Foursquare till January 2016 when he stepped aside in favour of Jeff Glueck, though Crowley continues to be involved in the company in his role as Executive Chairman.

Early Life

Born in Medway, Massachusetts on June 19, 1976 to Mary Moraski Crowley and Dennis P. Crowley, the future internet champ grew up in a close-knit family that revelled in humour and games. According to an online diary, titled Teendrama, that Crowley kept as a teenager, even attending the Sunday service in church would become an opportunity to have fun, as the family would compete on who could manage the maximum number of handshakes during the singing of the hymn, "Peace be with you". Later in college,

Crowley and his friends would charge freshmen a cover at the door of bars and as the latter were not allowed access to alcohol. One such party, recalled Crowley later, led to them being busted by the police but not before they had made a neat 1600 USD. Not surprisingly this penchant for social games gave way to career in creating social networking sites.

After graduating from Xaverian Brothers High School in Westwood, Massachusetts in 1994, Crowley earned his B.A. in 1998 from Syracuse University's S.I. Newhouse School of Public Communications. There he became one of the first students to wire his dorm room with Ethernet. After graduating from Syracuse, Crowley joined Jupiter Communications to work as a researcher. In 2000, he moved on to mobile app provider Vindigo in the role of a product developer but barely a year later the firm was compelled to restructure their workforce and Crowley found himself staring at a pink slip. His troubles worsened when he was evicted too from his apartment, the same week. However the desire to learn more, made him enroll in the New York University's Tisch School of the Arts Interactive Telecommunications Program from where he earned his M.P.S. Master's degree in 2004.

Budding Entrepreneur

While still studying in the New York University, Crowley developed a mobile app named 'Dodgeball' together with another student Alex Rainert whom he had met at orientation where a few students were gathered around a video game. This was a location-based social networking software provider for mobile devices. Dodgeball allowed users to text location to the service, which then informed them of friends, potential dates, eating joints and other recreational options nearby. Not only this, with Dodgeball could even "check-in", to bars or restaurants by sending a text while their "friends", on the service would get a text with the location. Users could also accumulate points for checking in. Though crowd-sourced initially, soon Dodgeball became a hit with users as it was faster than the existing alternative CitySearch which would often take long-time to update. Such was the popularity of Dodgeball, that Google offered to acquire it and the deal went through in 2005. Though Crowley had been allowed to stay on with Dodgeball under the new management, he found working there as "incredibly frustrating" and eventually in April 2007, he left Google. Dodgeball was replaced by its new owners in February 2009 with an app known as succeeded by Google Latitude which too was discontinued in 2013.

Success with Foursquare

Crowley however was determined to create something that would remain his own. Together with Naveen Selvadurai, another software whiz, he developed an even more advanced version of Dodgeball in late 2008 and named it 'Foursquare'. The service was formally launched at SXSW next year. While Dodgeball used SMS technology to enable users to send in their location, Foursquare could take advantage of in-built GPS technology and other location apps in the newer smartphones and such devices. With the original Foursquare, users could not only look for restaurants, stores and movies in the vicinity but could even to "check in" to them and share their location with friends. However in the Foursquare version 8.0 which was launched on August 7, 2014, the check-in and location sharing features were discarded and the service focused entirely on local search. The app supports languages like French, Italian, German, Spanish, Japanese as well as Indonesian, Korean, Portuguese, Russian and Thai. From June 2012 onwards, it started supporting Turkish as well.

As part of its continuing evolution, Foursquare improved its privacy policy in late December 2012. Under the updated privacy policy, users would be required to display their full names, instead of an initial for a surname.

Moreover companies would get a more detailed profile of visitors who check into their businesses over the day.

In the beginning of 2014, Foursquare managed to get some much-needed funding, primarily by investor Union Square Ventures. As part of the 45 million USD deal, Crowley relinquished his responsibilities to become an Executive Chairman while COO Jeff Glueck assumed the position of the CEO.

Success and Recognition

Crowley's success has been recognized both in financial and popular terms. For two consecutive years, 2010 and 2011, he figured on *fortune magazine's* "40 Under 40"—a list of top forty achievers below the age of forty. Even before that he had already been included in the MIT Technology Review "TR35", which profiled the top 35 innovators in the world under the age of 35.

Crowley however is not the kind of personality to remain content over a success. Though many offers of acquisition for Foursquare have come his way, he remained unwilling to let go of it. In the meantime, he continues to live according to the dictates of his inner voice, thinking up new things to do, create and explore.

□

14

Eduardo Saverin

Of Brazilian origin, Eduardo Saverin is a tech tycoon who is best known for co-founding with Mark Zuckerberg the most popular social networking site in the world, 'Facebook'. Though he has long exited from the management of the company, Saverin's stocks in Facebook has ensured that he will continue to be counted among the wealthiest internet billionaires of the world. Saverin's net worth, as of June, 2016, was 6.9 billion USD, making him not only one of the richest digital entrepreneurs but among the youngest too.

Early Life

Born as Eduardo Luiz Saverin on 19 March 1982 in Sao Paulo, the future internet billionaire was fortunate to have a comfortable childhood as the youngest of three sons of wealthy parents. In 1993, Saverin moved with his family to the United States and settled in Miami. There he studied at the Gulliver Preparatory School and proved to be a brilliant student. Not many are aware that when just thirteen years of age, Saverin defeated a chess grandmaster during a match in Orlando. In fact it was so unusual that he was mentioned on an article published by The *International Chess Magazine* and in this way made international headlines years before Facebook came into existence.

Not surprisingly for such a smart boy, he was accepted at Harvard University where while pursuing a degree in economics, he soon became a part of prestigious intellectual clubs like the Alpha Epsilon Pi Fraternity, the Phoenix S.K Club and even headed the Harvard Investment Association. This was early evidence of his knack for investment sense and in fact while still at Harvard, he funded as much as 300,000 USD in an oil venture.

Birth of an Internet Sensation

In 2006, Saverin graduated magna-cum-laude from Harvard University but instead of becoming an employee somewhere, he was already planning to invest in a venture that would go on to become an internet sensation. At Harvard, Saverin had met Mark Zuckerberg, then a sophomore, and had been impressed by the latter's vision of a site which would bring vast numbers of users into a web of connections.

In 2004 Facebook finally went live. While Zuckerberg continued to look after its technical aspect, Saverin took up the responsibility of managing the site's business aspect.

Trouble Ahead

However as Facebook continued to expand its business (within the first ten months of its existence, it garnered 1 million users), one trouble emerged between the two main founders. Saverin fell out with the management at Facebook who accused him of interfering with the business and even slapped a case on the co-founder. Another reason why Saverin attracted criticism from the Board was apparently because of his insistence on keeping a 30 per cent stake in Facebook. However Saverin was not one to take things lying down and he countersued Facebook in response which had diluted his shares from 34.4 per cent to a mere 0.03 per cent. Eventually in order to avoid an ugly drawn out legal battle which in turn would have harmed the company's public image, the parties agreed to an out-of-court settlement. According to its terms, Saverin would receive around 5 per cent stake as well as the status of a co-founder on Facebook's website. In turn, he would have to sign a non-disclosure contract.

After Saverin won the lawsuit against Facebook, he sold off more than half the number of shares he held with the company to investors like Digital Sky Technologies and Sharespost. According to *Forbes*, these sales netted him a cool 2.8 billion USD. After 2012, when Facebook went public, Saverin continued to hold a little less that 2 per cent of the company's outstanding shares which equalled 53,133,360 shares and worth a total of $2.18 billion.

Towards Other Shores

In 2011 Saverin renounced his American citizenship in favour of the highly developed Asian city-state Singapore. Critics pointed out that the decision was made to avoid paying high taxes in the United States. In contrast Singapore has no capital gains taxes and the U.S. does not impose capital gains tax on the U.S. investments of non-resident aliens. Saverin in turn defended his decision purely on personal grounds of choice of lifestyle. He has since invested in technology startups like Qwiki and Jumio, which is the founder of the online payment company Netswipe. Other tech ventures which have benefited from Saverin's fundings are Crowdmob—a website that promotes apps—as well as ShopSavvy, an app that provides shopping services.

In recent times, Saverin has been seen moving towards investing in philanthropic initiatives. In 2010 Saverin co-founded 'Aporta' with Mexican entrepreneur Aldo Alvarez, an online portal for charity. He has also expressed a desire to invest in Brazil, his country of origin, though he clarifies that any such venture needs to be technology based. Among his latest ventures are the news website known as 'Tech' in Asia, an airport car rental service named 'Silvercar' as well as an online retailer of kidswear in India, branded under the name 'Hopscotch'.

Eduardo Saverin's involvement with Facebook was cinematically captured in the 2010 box office success. The Social Network where he is depicted as Zuckerberg's good friend and business partner by actor Andrew Garfield for which the latter even received nominations such as the Golden Globe Award for best supporting Actor-Motion Picture and BAFTA Award for best actor in a supporting role. However the movie did not meet with complete approval from Saverin who dismissed the portrayal as a mere "Holloywood Fantasy".

On June 25, 2015, Saverin got married to Elaine Andriejanssen, a businesswoman with Chinese and Indonesian heritage at the exotic locales of French Riviera. The couple continues to reside in Singapore in a sprawling multi-million dollar penthouse in one of the richest neighbourhoods of the city. In his new life, Saverin seems to have made peace with his past. In a May 2012 interview to Brazilian newspaper *Veja*, he said about his Facebook co-founder, "I have only good things to say about Mark, there are no hard feelings between us. His focus on the company since its very first day is anything short of admirable. He was a visionary..." and about the company that catapulted him to international fame and wealth, Saverin revealed "Facebook's biggest strength, what allowed us to transform it into an instrument of protest, like what happened in Egypt, but also in an instrument of business, not to mention a way of naturally connecting with friends."

□

15

Eric Lefkofsky

Eric Lefkofsky is an American internet entrepreneur who is best known for co-founding 'Groupon', an e-commerce company that offers heavy discounts to consumers on the basis of a group discount model. Lefkofsky's stocks in Groupon as well as other investments have helped him to enjoy a net worth of $1.37 billion, as of July 2016, according to Forbes.com.

Early Life

Eric Lefkofsky was born on September 2, 1969 in Detroit, Michigan but grew up in Southfield in the same state. His father was a structural engineer while his mother was a school teacher. Young Eric attended Southfield-Lathrup High School from where he passed out in 1987.

After high school, Lefkofsky enrolled in the University of Michigan from where he earned his bachelor's degree in 1991. He next proceeded to the Law School of the same university to receive his Juris Doctor in 1993.

Budding Entrepreneur

While still in his freshman year, Lefkofsky made his earliest foray into business-reportedly after a girlfriend left him—and he began selling carpets. More importantly this was also the time when he got to know Brad Keywell, a college mate, who would turn out to be his business partner of many ventures in the future.

Among the first of these joint ventures was a clothing company named Brandon Apparel that Lefkofsky and Keywell bought after leaving college in 1993 from Madison, Wisconsin after raising money from relatives. Next they founded an Internet company called 'Starbelly' that offered promotional products to companies. Though Starbelly experienced rapid growth and even found a buyer in Halo Industries in January 2000, with the bursting of the dot com bubble, it went bankrupt.

Soon however Lefkofsky rallied back with the launching of yet another company InnerWorkings, Inc. in the fall of 2001. This was a provider of print procurement services for mid-sized companies and proved to be much more successful in the long run, with a respectable initial public offering too on NASDAQ in August 2006. Lefkofsky would continue to remain on the board of directors of InnerWorkings until October 2012.

Lefkofsky and Keywell together created two more startups—Echo Logistics and MediaBank—before they came on board of a project started by another internet entrepreneur Andrew Mason. This was Point.com, a website that encouraged collective action to support various causes. When Mason saw that many of the site's most successful projects brought users together to acquire buying power, he got the idea to spin off a commercial site on the same logic. This was initially known as 'getyourgroupon.com' and to launch this, Mason roped in Lefkofsky and Keywell. Eventually the site came to be known as 'Groupon.com'—a fusion of the words 'group' and 'coupon' and was properly launched in 2008.

Success with Groupon

Groupon was designed as a group discount site where users were encouraged to sign up for deals on a variety of products and services which could range from dining out and car tune-ups to spa packages and theatre tickets. Once a pre-determined level of purchases would be reached—which could vary on a per-case basis—the deal would be made official. This was done to make the discount potentially profitable for the vendor. After an offer was made official, the customers would be charged, and the "Groupon" appear in their account. Customers could either printout their offers and present them to the vendor or display the vouchers on digital devices like mobile phones.

The founders also encouraged users to share Groupon offers with their friends through e-mail or social networking sites so as to reach the requisite number of sales. The source of Groupon's revenue was the percentage they got from the proceeds, often around half the sale price. In 2011 the company also started offering "Groupon Now!" deals, which were generally offered on the day of purchase and that too for a short span of time. The site later added sections for purchasing discounted vacations and high-value goods.

Within just seven months of its launch, Groupon turned out profitable. Though it was started in Chicago, where it was also headquartered, the company quickly expanded to other major cities during this time, including Boston, New York, and Washington, D.C. and in less than two years of it going live, it had expanded its presence to more than 150 cities in the United States as well as to more than 30 countries around the world.

By early 2011 more than 30 million offers were claimed by customers using the Group network. As a mark of its phenomenal success, the company decided to raise funding in November 2011 and managed to attract $700 million through its initial public offering which turned out to be the largest by an Internet company since Google Inc.'s $1.66 billion IPO in 2004.

However 2012 saw Groupon struggling to keep up its revenues and by August its stock had dived down by 75 per cent. In February 2013, Lefkofsky was brought in to replace

Mason as the CEO. However in November 2015, Groupon's board voted to bring in COO Rich Williams in place of Lefkofsky who though continued to remain Chairman.

Other Ventures

In recent times, Lefkofsky has remained busy with other ventures. Together with his long time partner Brad Keywell, he owns 15 per cent of the historic Wrigley Building in downtown Chicago.

The duo has also gone on to start Lightbank, a Chicago-based venture capital firm which has a current portfolio of more than 60 companies including Beachmint, a e-commerce site as well as Belly, a customer rewards program.

□

16
Evan Spiegel

Evan Spiegel is an American internet entrepreneur who shot to fame after he co-founded the hugely popular messaging app, 'Snapchat''. He enjoyed a net worth of 2.1 billion USD, as of May 2016, which is just as well since Spiegel has often been in the news for his lavish partying ways. Despite something of the wild-child reputation that he has acquired, Spiegel has been widely hailed for his successful ventures which have made him—at 26 years age—one of the youngest billionaires in present times.

Early Life

Born as Evan Thomas Spiegel on June 4, 1990 to Ivy League-educated attorneys, he has been fortunate to grow up in comfortable circumstances. Both his parents—mother, Melissa Ann Thomas and father, John W. Spiegel—were successful lawyers and ensured that their son got the best that money could buy. Consequently Evan went to an expensive private school, Crossroads School of Arts and Sciences, in Santa Monica, California and while still in high school he took design classes at the Otis College of Art and Design. After graduating from high school, he joined Stanford University, his father's *alma mater*, but not before he did a stint at the Art Center College of Design in Pasadena, the preceding summer.

At Stanford, Spiegel continued with his passion for contemporary arts and majored in product design. Along with a strong creative streak, Spiegel was also blessed with social skills. While at high school, he often threw parties and later at Stanford became the social chair of his Kappa Sigma fraternity. Also there he networked extensively and managed to meet with influential people like Eric Schmidt, executive chairman of Google. An even more consequential meeting was with Scott Cook, co-founder and chairman of the executive committee of Intuit, who offered Spiegel a job at the tech company even before the young man had completed his degree.

Budding Entrepreneur

Completing a degree at Stanford however did not happen for Spiegel. As part of the curriculum, Spiegel was required to submit a class project and this led to the birth of Snapchat. In fact, according to a media report, it was a conversation on risqué texting language between Spiegel and his frat-mates, Frank Reginald Brown and Bobby Murphy, that resulted in the smartphone app which allows users to send disappearing pictures to their contacts. Initially it was named 'Picaboo' upon a suggestion from Brown, but investors could not see any value in funding an app which deletes pictures that have been posted by users. Eventually Brown exited the group while the remaining duo settled for the name 'Snapchat'.

The app quickly caught on the imagination of young users with its innovative features. The images or short videos known as 'snaps' could be viewed for a user-specified length of time which ranged from 1 to 10 seconds before they became inaccessible. Also users could send 'snaps' privately to their contacts or to a semi-public Story. In case of the latter, users at a specific location—like a music concert or sporting event-could send photos that was then advertised to all users, in the process, curating a common story but which was visible from varied angles of the contributors.

Though it was launched from Spiegel's dorm-room, it went on to become so popular that Spiegel was forced to leave Stanford just a few credits short of graduating and devote himself full time to Snapchat.

However with success, came certain problems. Frank Reginald Brown, alleged that he was a co-founder of the company but was being cut out by Spiegel and his team—seeking redress, he went to court and demanded a 20 per cent stake in Snapchat. Spiegel in turn sought legal advice but in order to avoid a lengthy legal battle, both sides agreed to an out-of-court settlement in September 2014.

Also owning to Snapchat's immense popularity, the app has attracted acquisition bids—the most famous being an offer from Facebook for a reported sum of 3 billion USD. However like Facebook's founder Zuckerberg himself, Spiegel has remained staunchly resistant to any such bids. In May 2015, Snapchat received a funding to the tune of 538 million USD and consequently it was valued at around 16 billion USD.

Though it started as a personal messaging app, Snapchat has over time taken on public content as well and now includes brand networks, publications as well as live events like music and sports. In January 2015, a feature called 'Discover' was added which showed channels of ad-supported short-form content from bigger publishers like BuzzFeed, CNN, ESPN, Mashable, People and Vice.

Personal Life

Growing up in highly privileged section of society, Spiegel was never a stranger to the good life. And with Snapchat's success, he has continued to live it up amidst the luxurious environs of Los Angeles where Snapchat is headquartered. His love for snazzy cars, private vacations, high-end partying and Hollywood beauties has for a long time kept the paparazzi happy.

However he bore the brunt of his playboy image when in May 2014, the tech blog 'Valleywag' published e-mails that Spiegel had sent during his college days. Apart from being explicit, these were clearly misogynistic and homophobic, and Spiegel was compelled to apologize for them. In an e-mail to Business Insider, he wrote about the leaks, "I'm obviously mortified and embarrassed that my idiotic e-mails during my fraternity days were made public. I have no excuse...I'm sorry I wrote them at the time and I was jerk to have written them. They in no way reflect who I am today or my views towards women."

Currently Spiegel is reported to be dating supermodel Miranda Kerr. He is also soaking in the success of his venture—Snapchat is estimated to be used by around 100 million people daily and it has been estimated that as high as 60 per cent of American smartphone users in the 13-34 age group are on this free service.

□

17

Evan Williams

When was the last time you dashed out 140 characters to update your status, voice your opinion or follow someone? Chances are, not very long back. This is what Twitter is all about, the social networking and microblogging site that has become extremely popular and was co-founded in 2006 by Evan Williams and Biz Stone. Williams the director of Twitter today and worth more than 1.8 billion USD even though he owns just over 6 per cent of the company's stock.

Early Life

Born Evan Clark Williams on March 31, 1972 in the small town of Clarks, Nebraska, the future internet sensation actually grew up in a farming family. Evan was the third child of Monte Williams and Laurie Howe Williams and like other members of his family, grew up working on their corn and soybean farm.

In order to follow his aspirations of life outside a farm, Williams enrolled into the University of Nebraska at Lincoln but after a year and half, dropped out without getting his degree. Instead he decided to pursue a career in the newly emerging field of information systems. This took him to places like at Key West in Florida as well as Dallas and Austin in Texas where he took up various technology jobs with startup firms. For a short while he returned to his family farm in Nebraska but then in 1996, left for Sebastopol,

California in Sonoma County to work for the technology publishing company O'Reilly Media. Though Williams joined the firm in a marketing position, soon his bent for technology prompted him to become an independent contractor writing computer code.

Budding Entrepreneur

As a freelancer, Williams wrote computer code for companies like Hewlett-Packard and Intel. During this time he came across tech whiz Meg Hourihan and the two together founded Pyra Labs for the original purpose of making project management software. A note-taking feature on this led to the creation of Blogger—one of the earliest applications for writing and managing short journals for the web, which was initially known as weblogs and then by its abbreviated version, blog. In fact Williams was largely responsible for coming up with the term 'blogger' and popularizing the activity as blogging. The team that created Blogger—Williams and two friends, sold it to Google on February 13, 2003. Williams started working for Google after this but the entrepreneurial streak in him never stopped ticking and he left after two years with the company.

In 2004 Williams founded the podcast company Odeo. The very next year, Biz Stone—a friend and Blogger co-founder—joined Odeo as well. Shortly after they came across another software engineer, Jack Dorsey, who had been exploring the possibilities of using the principles of dispatch software to develop text messaging and instant messaging as a way of social networking. Together they developed a prototype of what would become the Twitter platform. In 2006, Williams co-founded the Obvious Corporation with Biz Stone, Jack Dorsey and Noah Glass to acquire all previous properties from Odeo's former backers.

This became the team that eventually built the Twitter, as it was then called. This took the shape of an online social-networking and micro-blogging site that allowed users to post short messages of 140 characters or less, known as "tweets" in real time. Seeing the popularity of the site, the founder's team decided to spin Twitter itself into a new company in April 2007. While Williams was already a co-founder, he now became board member and investor as well. Designated as the first Chairman of Twitter, Williams provided much of the financing for the company during this time. In October 2008, Williams and Dorsey exchanged roles—while Williams took on the responsibilities of a CEO, Dorsey in turn became the Chairman at Twitter. Williams would go on to run the company for two years, from 2008 to 2010.

Under Williams' stewardship, Twitter rapidly became popular all over the globe. By 2012, it boasted of 500 million registered users who tweeted approximately 340 million messages each day. Not surprisingly, Twitter Inc.-headquartered in San Francisco and with offices in New York City, Boston, San Antonio and Detroit, went public in November 2013, and was listed as TWTR at New York Stock Exchange. At this time, the 12 per cent stake held by Williams in the company worth was 1.5 billion USD, according to the October 2013 Securities Exchange Commission.

Recent Initiatives

Though Williams continues to be the Director at Twitter, in recent years he has reduced his involvement in the day-to-day running of the company. Instead his time and energy are now taken by Medium, the online publishing platform that he founded in 2012 with long-time business partner and one of Twitter co-founders, Biz Stone. Backed by Obvious Corp., this is a no-frills site where bloggers can share ideas and stories including graphics, without the limitation of 140 characters.

Currently, Williams lives in San Francisco with his wife, Sara, and their two sons. In 2003, his name was included in MIT Technology Review magazine's "Top 100 innovators under age 35" list. Again next year, he was feted by the PC Magazine as the "Person of the Year", for his work on Blogger.

In recent times, Williams' views on Twitter, social networking and the internet in general have garnered a lot of attention. In 2007, while giving an interview to MIT Technology Review, Williams called Twitter "a no-brainer" for "social animals." "People like other people," he stated. "So hearing from them, and being able to express yourself to people you care about in a really simple way, is fun, and it can be addictive." Again in a September 2013 interview with Wired.com, Williams said in the same vein, "We often think of the internet enables you to do new things. But people just want to do the same things they've always done." He later added, "Convenience on the internet is basically achieved by two things: speed, and cognitive ease ... The internet is not what I thought it was 20 years ago. It's not a utopian world. It's essentially like a lot of other major technological revolutions that have taken place in the history of the world."

Despite Williams' own realistic views on the Internet and social networking sites, Twitter has emerged as a powerful opinion maker around the world. During the 2008 presidential elections in the United States, both candidates—Barack Obama and John McCain—used the website to update their supporters while on the campaign trail. Globally it came under the spotlight in 2009—with the government of Iran blocking text-messaging and satellite feeds of foreign news coverage during presidential elections in the Middle Eastern nation that year, tweeting emerged as one of the most effective ways of getting information in and out of the country.

□

18
Gary Kremen

What started out as the last resort to getting a date on a Saturday evening has now become an integral part of mainstream culture—online dating is here to stay. And the portal that pioneered, it is the vastly popular dating site, 'Match.com' that reputedly earned over $450 million in revenue in 2011. However the brain behind it all was that of American engineer and entrepreneur, Gary Kremen who incredibly founded the world's biggest online dating site and then gave it up after just two years. Though Kremen is no longer part of Match.com, he continues to be an inspiration of entrepreneurs across the world who are not afraid to chart new territories. Today Kremen remains busy funding a whole variety of startups, both individually and through venture capital funds and currently serves as the Chair of Santa Clara Valley Water District.

Early Life

Not much is known about Gary Kremen's initial years. He is believed to have been brought up in Chicago—he attended Northwestern University and in 1989 graduated from Stanford Business School. Right from his college days, Kremen had a reputation for unconventionality. According to an anecdote, though he was found brilliant enough to be invited for a summer internship at reputed investment firm Goldman Sachs, just after three weeks, one of the firm's partners offered to pay up the remainder of Kremen's internship if the young man left—this was presumably due to Kremen's disruptive ways which was thought to have a bad influence on the rest of the company's employees.

Budding Entrepreneur

After graduating from Stanford University, Kremen started two software companies which did not turn out to be very successful. In the meantime, his own experiences in personal life made him aware of the huge potential of an Internet-based dating service. At the time, options to find a partner were limited to newspaper personals as well as video and telephone dating services. And as Kremen himself began shelling out $2.99 per minute on 900-number dating services, he realized that this together with personals and video ads was bound to be too expensive for the common man, not to speak of time-consuming and complication.

It was around this time that Kremen began thinking of putting together a personals database on the internet. However in 1993, the internet was still a relatively new medium and potential investors were wary of its reach, efficacy and viability. Though Kremen had the larger vision of launching online personals database across various categories such as housing, jobs and cars, he decided to start with a dating classifieds as he believed this would make it easier to attract users and investors alike. Thus in 1993, Kremen founded Electric Classifieds Inc (ECI) with the aim of starting a series of online personals database. The following year, ECI managed to convince angel investors and a few venture-capital firms to cough up around 1.5 million USD in funding. Canaan Partners being the primary investor. Finally April 1995, Match.com went live and thus became one of the earliest dating websites on the internet.

Match.com turned out to be an instant success—primarily because Kremen had the foresight of making the dating site attractive to women. He knew that once women began frequenting, the paying male users would follow. In fact in the heady days of its success, the dating site sometimes experienced a growth rate as high as three to four per cent per day.

However with success, came complexities. The ECI Board wanted the company to primarily serve the major newspapers with its software platform providing back-end technology to clients who wanted to post their existing classifieds online. However Kremen's whimsical and impetuous nature was completely out of place in the tardy, bureaucratic world of newspapers' operations.

Besides the board found the dating services by Match.com unsavoury and wanted to delink ECI with personal classifieds. Kremen could do nothing about this short-sightedness since his own style of rash, short-tempered management often put him at loggerheads with the Board. Eventually Kremen was asked to give up the post of the CEO though he continued to be on the ECI Board. A replacement was found in Richard Neustadt—a down-to-earth genuine leader who Kremen himself approved of. However in a tragic turn of events, Neustadt died in a rafting accident just the weekend before he was to join ECI. The following two CEOs proved to be unsuitable for the job and eventually in 1997 the Board—in yet another short-sighted move—decided to sell off Match.com to Connecticut based consumer services company, Cendant for a mere $7 million. Though Kremen did his all to oppose the sale, he was outruled by the Board. The major error by the Board was brought home when just a year and half later, Cendant sold Match.com to Ticketmaster CitySearch services for a whopping $50 million. Kremen was left with just $50,000 in cash from the sale of Match.com that he had envisioned and founded. Incredibly he even lost his girlfriend.

Later Ventures

However the mark of a true visionary is that he cannot

be kept down for long. Though Kremen did not gain much financially from Match.com, the knowledge that he had the ability to spot emerging trends in technology and internet as well as give shape to a vision proved invaluable. Equally important the experience taught him to stay away from day-to-day management roles. Backed by this new-acquired awareness, Kremen took up the ideation and funding of several projects in the following years. Among these the most successful has been Clean Power Finance (CPF). The company provides unique solutions to offset heavy installation costs to homeowners who plan to use clean energy in their daily living. In early September 2011, CPF attracted as much as 25 million USD in venture capital funding and its success seemed cemented when in the same month, internet search giant Google announced plans of pumping another $75 million in Kremen's company.

Today, Kremen enjoys a net worth of around $20 million—this may not seem as high as other internet billionaires of the Silicon Valley but what is important is that he remains true to his creative and wacky ways. A hardcore fan of the punk rock group Grateful Dead and at the same time heading Santa Clara Valley Water District as its Chairperson—a contrasting, colourful success that is quintessentially Gary Kremen.

□

19

Immad Akhund

Immad Akhund is a British internet entrepreneur who is most famous for co-founding the social game mobile app, known as 'Heyzap'. Akhund is the CEO of Heyzap as well and has radically changed the way people play games on mobile and smart devices.

Early Life

Akhund was born on 16 April 1984 in the Pakistani city of Karachi. With his family migrating to UK and settling in Harrow, London, he attended Nower Hill High School in Middlesex and Dr Challoner's Grammar School located in Amersham, Buckinghamshire. After passing out from school, he enrolled in the Clare College at University of Cambridge from where he graduated with a Bachelors degree in Computer Science.

Budding Entrepreneur

Akhund's first job after graduation was that of software engineer in Bloomberg L.P. which he joined in 2006. Here he stayed for a little more than one year and then left to launch his first startup, Revmap. This was an app that searched events and recreational places for the user. Though not very popular, the experience with Revmap convinced Akhund that the internet was the place to be—at the time he was only twenty-two.

Next Akhund launched new company called Clickpass in 2007 along with Peter Nixey. With this, users could create an Open ID, which could then be used as a single password to access various websites, including Hotmail, Yahoo, Google, Facebook, and AIM. With the internet being used more and more for commercial, business and official purposes, people now began to find it increasingly difficult to remember passwords of multiple websites and their accounts. Clickpass in turn would enable a user to log on to all of their sites, so that he or she would have to remember the security details for just one website instead of multiple ones.

To make Clickpass popular, Akhund entered into partnership with Plaxo, Scribd, Disqus and other such websites. In the first few weeks itself, the service saw 1,000 people sign up every day. As the CEO and co-founder of the company, Akhund had to look around for investors and with this in mind, he moved to San Francisco which was a hub of the internet revolution. In the summer of 2007, he attended the reputed Y Combinator round to attract seed-funding for his startup, which too was now based in Wilmington, Delaware. Clickpass caught the interest of Yola Inc which acquired it on December 18, 2008, for an undisclosed sum.

Success with Heyzap

With the acquisition of Clickpass, Akhund was now free to dream up the next big thing. This turned out to be the social gaming website, Heyzap, that he co-founded with his childhood friend Jude Gomila in 2009. Based in San Francisco again, Heyzap was successful in attracting funding from Y Combinator and Union Square Ventures as well as angel investors such as Naval Ravikant and Chris Dixon.

Originally Heyzap offered a widget service for embedding flash games based on the internet. Subsequently it expanded to include a virtual goods platform for flash games which enabled developers to insert microtransaction systems into their games so that games could become profitable commecially.

In April 2010, Heyzap went through further changes, with the addition of social games and an Arcade Bar. Flush with the 3 million USD it was able to raise, the company launched a cool new Heyzap Arcade.

Next year around the same time, Akhund launched the mobile avatar of Heyzap with attractive social discovery features. Now one could not only play games with their 'friends' and other users, but could also discover games and join an exhaustive community of mobile gamers. Besides these, users could compete on leader-boards, challenge 'friends' as well as earn special rewards and badges.

In March 2013, Akhund and his team brought about a major overhaul in Heyzap. The app now having its own advertising network focused on mobile games. Soon the advertising platform became the biggest source of revenue for Heyzap and thus the main focus of the company from the business point of view. As part of its advertising function, interstitial, video and cross-promotion were some of the multiple formats offered by Heyzap. In keeping with Akhund's constant search for innovation, Heyzap became the first mobile ad network to use bitcoin—the digital currency—to make payments.

The success of Heyzap is no longer in doubt. Running both on Android and iOS, the app has totalled around six million installs. It has found the secret of its success with enabling people discover games as well as play them with their friends. According to its own estimate, it has been integrated into 5,000 mobile games and apps as of April 2014 and is reported to have a revenue run rate of more than 13 million USD, making Heyzap one of the most successful mobile gaming apps in the current scenario.

Akhund's success with Heyzap appeared to be acknowledged in the market too as in December 2015, Berlin-based mobile advertising technology company RNTS bagged it for a whopping 45 million USD.

Currently Akhund remains busy with speaking engagements across the world where he talks about social and mobile gaming. He also blogs regularly about startups and online ventures. Apart from these, he is an advisor for Seedcamp which provides funding for potential and fledgling startups. In recognition of his role in co-founding Heyzap as well as making it flourish as its CEO, Akhund was named in the prestigious 30 Under 30 List Of 2012 released by Inc Magazine. Giving the example of his own successive ventures and eventual success, Akhund encourages young entrepreneurs to work with passion and think up innovative ideas.

□

20
Jack Ma

Jack Ma can be profitably described as the headline of the Internet success story that is sweeping China. He is not only the richest Chinese today with an estimated net worth of more than $23 billion but is the pioneer of e-commerce in a country whose economy was for many decades restricted by communist ideology. Ma's fame and wealth largely rests on the spectacular success of the Alibaba Group, an umbrella company of several Internet-based businesses that he founded and of which he continues to serve as the Executive Chairman. When Alibaba went public in 2014, it created history as the biggest IPO in the world till date, doing a business worth a whopping $150 billion. Today the Alibaba Group has nine major subsidiaries: Alibaba.com, Taobao Marketplace, Tmall, eTao, Alibaba Cloud Computing, Juhuasuan, 1688.com, AliExpress.com and Alipay.

Early life

Born as Ma Yun on September 10, 1964 in Hangzhou, in the southeastern part of China, Jack Ma grew up in a time when China was still shut off from western culture and market economy. His parents were traditional musicians and his family consisted of an elder brother and a younger sister. Despite his diminutive size, Ma Yun was enterprising from an early age. Eager to learn English, he showed tourists around in his hometown and even made friends with visitors from other countries. This was in the aftermath of US President Richard Nixon's visit to Hangzhou in 1972 which put the city in the tourist map of the world. In fact, it was through one such association that he got his nickname—Jack—named by a foreigner who found it too difficult to pronounce the boy's traditional Chinese name.

Formal education however was not accessible so easily to Jack Ma. Though he finished high school, he had difficulty getting into a college. After having failed entrance examinations to college twice, Ma proved successful the third time when he was accepted in Hangzhou Teacher's Institute. He graduated from this institute in 1988 and in order to become financially independent began looking for jobs. Once again he was faced with repeated rejections—one of the most notable being the global fast-food brand KFC. Eventually Ma was able to land a job in a university where he was required to teach English. Though the pay was a meagre $12 a month, the young teacher quickly became popular with his students. It was also around this time that he met Zhang Ying, his future wife.

Budding Entrepreneur

With his language skills and natural bent for entrepreneurship, it was only a matter of time before Ma started his own business. This was a translation venture that further opened up the world to him. In 1995 Ma visited the US in order to recover a payment for a Chinese client. Apart from being his first overseas trip, the US visit proved momentous in another very important way—it introduced him to the fascinating world of internet and made him aware of its immense commercial possibilities. According to an anecdote, when Ma searched "beer" while using the Internet, he was puzzled to find that the search results did not turn up any Chinese company. Eventually he decided to start his own internet-based company in China and this paved the way for Alibaba.

Even then, success did not come easy to Ma. His first two ventures did not do well and not surprisingly he had a difficult time, getting investors for his third project. But he finally managed to get together around seventeen friends in his apartment and convince them to support his plans for the first online marketplace in China. Thus Alibaba was born as a site that enabled Chinese exporters to post their product listings and sell to customers globally.

From Strength to Strength

Soon the online marketplace became so popular that buyers and sellers from other parts of the world began using the service regularly. This helped it to get investment from major financiers like Goldman Sachs which pumped in $20 million as well as SoftBank, a Japan-based telecom company which shored up Ma's startup with another $5 million. By October 1999 thus Alibaba was on firm footing and clearly a success.

However this was also a time when the e-commerce scene was getting hotter with the entry of many players, among which some like e-Bay were often responsible for pushing the smaller ones into extinction. When Ma's Alibaba was similarly threatened with the arrival of e-Bay in China in the early 2000s, he decided to launch a nifty competitor named, Taobao.

Eventually a bigger success came in 2005 when Yahoo agreed to invest $1 billion in Alibaba in exchange for about a 40 per cent stake in the company. This proved to be a win-win situation for both sides as on one hand it enabled Ma to withstand competition from global ecommerce giants like e-Bay and on the other, it returned Yahoo a massive $10 billion when Alibaba went public in September 2014. The company's initial public offering turned out to be the largest in the economic history of the United States, garnering $25 billion for the company. This made Alibaba one of the most valuable tech companies of the world and its founder, Jack

Ma the wealthiest man in China. On that day, he announced, "Today what we got is not money. What we got is the trust from the people."

Legacy

To a large extent Ma's incredible financial success, is due to his forward looking ideas and belief in team work. Back in the days when Alibaba was still a fledgling company, Ma ensured that his employees could work in a trusting and highly motivated environment. He convinced his small team that they would survive, "We will make it because we are young and we never, never give up," equally he ensured that everybody working for him had a lot of fun as well-In fact, he is believed to have celebrated the first profits of his company by gifting each employee a can of Silly String to freak out with. Later during the days of tough competition, he apparently encouraged his employees to do handstands during breaks to maintain a sense of energy and optimism. Upon Alibaba's stupendous success at the IPO, Ma reminded his employees what the company stood for, saying that he hoped they would use their newfound wealth to become "A batch of genuinely noble people, a batch of people who are able to help others, and who are kind and happy."

Jack Ma has himself led the way with several philanthropic initiatives, especially those which work to protect the environment. He is on the global board of the Nature Conservancy besides being the leading supporter of 27,000-acre nature reserve in China. Additionally he is deeply interested in the traditional Chinese practice of Tai-Chi and is a firm believer in its benefits for the mind and body. On the personal front, Ma has been lucky to be supported by a long marriage—he has two children, a daughter and a son, who is an undergrad at UC Berkeley. A firm believer in enterprise and hard work, Ma continues to encourage future generations in his own country and across the world to dream big, both for oneself and the community.

□

21

Jeff Bezos

Jeff Bezos is the founder and chief executive officer of e-commerce giant, 'Amazon.com'. He ushered in the tide of online retail and ensured that Amazon emerged as one of the biggest virtual marketplaces in the global economy. Not content with that, Bezos engineered the acquisition of 'The Washington Post', newspaper for $250 million and later went on to spearhead innovations like Prime Air Amazon which uses drones for product delivery. As of June 2016 Bezos enjoyed a net worth of around 63.3 billion USD and was ranked fourth on the *Forbes* list of billionaires.

Early Life

Jeff Bezos was born on January 12, 1964, in Albuquerque, New Mexico. At the time of his birth his mother Jacklyn Gise Jorgensen was still a teenager. Her marriage to Jeff's biological father, Ted Jorgensen ended within a year after which she married Cuban immigrant Mike Bezos.

Even as a child, Jeff showed his aptitude for technology and science. He converted his parents' garage into a laboratory and set up electrical gadgets around his house—in fact there is an anecdote about how as just a boy, he rigged up an electric alarm to keep out his younger siblings out of his room. Young Jeff's passion for technology found an academic outlet in the study of computers in which he excelled at high school. At the same time, his knack for entrepreneurship was evident in the way he started his first business—The Dream Institute, an educational summer camp for fourth, fifth and sixth graders when he was still a high school student. No wonder then that he graduated high school as valedictorian and then continued his successful streak at Princeton University, where he graduated summa cum laude in 1986 with a degree in computer science and electrical engineering.

Jeff's first job after graduating from Princeton was at Fitel, a startup that was building a network to further global financial trades. After working for two years there, he moved to Bankers Trust and put in around the same amount of time. It was then that he received a call from investment firm D.E. Shaw where he soon proved his mettle, becoming the youngest employee to reach the position of vice president in 1990. However even such a meteoric rise could not satisfy him for long and the fast expanding world of internet caught his attention. One day in May 1994, sitting at the computer in his 39th-floor office in midtown Manhattan, Bezos was struck by the fact that the Internet was growing at a staggering rate of 2,300 per cent a year. He later said of the eureka moment, "It was a wake-up call...I started thinking, O.K., what kind of business opportunity might there be here?"

Birth of a Giant

In answer, the 30-year-old left his lucrative job at D. E. Shaw, moved to Seattle and decided to tap in the as-yet unexplored potential of the internet to run a business. After having researched the Top 20 mail-order products, Bezos realized that the market lack any popular mail-order books catalogues for the simple reason that good catalogue needed to include thousands of listings—something that would be too expensive for mail order listings but just right for the internet with its virtually limitless scope of conveying information. Thus Bezos decided on an online bookstore and then set about learning the book business as fast as he could. Whatever he found out only strengthened his resolve to try his hand at e-commerce and after having convinced family and friends to sponsor his project, Bezos set up his nascent company in his garage. There, aided by a small team, he began developing the software needed to run an e-commerce site. Soon enough the operations expanded to include three Sun Microstations in a two-bedroom house and eventually into a test site. In order to beta test the site, Bezos invited 300 friends after which Amazon.com was officially launched on July 16, 1995.

The site became an immediate hit. Within just a month and without any media publicity, Amazon.com sold books across the United States and in 45 other countries. In the next two months, sales touched $20,000 a week—far more than any estimate that Bezos and his startup team had made. Not surprisingly, Amazon.com went public in 1997 and attracted foremost investors of the day. Bezos was careful to keep diversifying the products sold at the site—from books, Amazon.com moved on to offer CDs and videos in 1998, and then, electronics, toys and lifestyle products through major retail partnerships. This was one of the major reasons, why Amazon was able to weather the dotcom bust that finished off many of the startups of the early '90s. Amazon not only survived but actually flourished with yearly sales shooting up from $510,000 in 1995 to over $17 billion in 2011.

Expanding Vision

In recent years, Bezos has expanded Amazon from an online store to a brand with multiple offerings. In 2006, Amazon.com launched its video on demand service which eventually came to be known as 'Amazon Instant Video'. The very next year came one of the Amazon's most popular products the 'Kindle', a digital book reader that users could hold in their hands and read like the traditional paper book.

This offered the additional advantage of buying, downloading and storing huger book selections. That same year, Bezos also invested in a Seattle-based aerospace company called 'Blue Space' that promotes commercial space travel. In 2011, Amazon entered the highly competitive world of tablets with its 'Kindle Fire', which was soon followed by the next generation 'Kindle Fire HD', designed to take Apple's iPad head on. "We haven't built the best tablet at a certain price. We have built the best tablet at any price," Bezos later said about the product during an interview to ABC News. With the takeover of 'The Washington Post' and other affiliated publications on August 5, 2013, Bezos made a definitive entry into traditional print media. When this led to concerns over the changing values and mechanics of journalism, he assured employees saying, "We will need to invent, which means we will need to experiment". Our touchstone will be readers, understanding what they care about—government, local leaders, restaurant openings, scout troops, businesses, charities, governors, sports—and working backwards from there. I'm excited and optimistic about the opportunity for invention."

The same enthusiasm for inventions resurfaced in 2013 when Bezos unveiled plans for using remote-controlled aerial machines to deliver Amazon products to its customers, 'Named Amazon Air Prime'. Bezos revealed that these drones could carry items weighing up to five pounds, and could cover a 10-mile radius from the company's distribution centre—In fact he was optimistic that Amazon Air Prime could be actually used in as little as three to four years. However in the following year, Bezos expansionist impulses received a check when Amazon's entry into the raging smartphone market, named the Fire Phone, was roundly planned and was quickly withdrawn. Even then he continued to look for other tie-ups. In keeping with this, he launched 'Amazon Studios' which in recent times has developed critically acclaimed original content like Transparent and

Mozart in the Jungle as well as Spike Lee's Chi-Raq as its first original feature film.

In his personal life, Bezos prefers to remain out of the public gaze. He is married to Mackenzie, also a graduate from Princeton University but whom he met while working at Shaw. An English-literature major, Mackenzie had worked as Toni Morrison's assistant and was crucial in supporting Bezos' decision to start Amazon. The couple have four children and continue to live in Seattle, Washington.

Despite his huge net worth, Bezos is reputed to take home one of the lowest salaries among the CEOs of the largest tech companies in the world. According to a 2013 story on Bloomberg.com, he took home an annual salary of $81,840 in 2012. However he says that money for money's sake does not attract him at all. The pioneer of online retail would much rather keep exploring unchartered territories in commerce and technology.

□

22
Jeffrey Skoll

Jeffrey Skoll is a Canadian internet billionaire, film producer and philanthropist. He is best known as the first employee and president of the online auction site, eBay which has revolutionized the way people all over the world buy and sell products as well as services. As of July 2016, Skoll enjoyed a net worth of 4.3 billion USD according to Forbes.com. He has used a large part of his wealth for charitable initiatives, especially through the 'Skoll Foundation' and his media company 'Participant Media'.

Early Life

Born in Canadian Jewish family of Montreal, on January 16, 1965, Skoll grew up initially in the Francophone culture of Quebec. While his mother taught in school, his father owned a firm that sold industrial chemicals. After his family moved to Toronto in the late 1970s, Skoll flourished in the cosmopolitan culture of the city. However tragedy struck and Skoll's father was diagnosed with liver cancer. In an interview with Thomas Watson for Canadian Business, Skoll recalled that incident having a profound impact on him, "I remember my Dad saying that he wasn't so sad that he might die, but he was sad that he'd never done the things that he'd wanted to do in life". This convinced Skoll not only to follow his passion as a career but eventually played a determining role in his emergence as a philanthropist. Again his decision to leave eBay at the heights of his success could be traced back to this time when he realized that money was not the same thing as a healthy life and should never become the only reason for a particular lifestyle.

After completing high school, Skoll enrolled into University of Toronto from where he earned a degree in electrical engineering in 1987. However money was scarce during these years and he reportedly had to work as a gas attendant in North York, Ontario to pay for his college tuition. Upon graduating, Skoll set off with a backpack, visiting many different parts of the world for several months. He returned to Canada refreshed with new ideas which was evident from the two new ventures he set up in Toronto. One of these was Skoll Engineering that offered information technology consultancy services while the other was a computer rental firm named.

However in 1993, Skoll received Masters of Business Administration degree at Stanford Business School, for which he moved to the United States. The sight of homeless people and absence of universal healthcare here surprised Skoll who was used to the far more comprehensive social services network in Canada. Even as a student, Skoll decided to do something about it and after he became editor of the Stanford business school student's newspaper, *The Reporter*, he started highlighting the gap between the rich and the poor in the world, and what fresh business school graduates like him could do to narrow it down.

After graduating from Stanford in 1995, Skoll took up a position with the publisher, Knight-Ridder where he was given the responsibility of designing new internet projects for the company.

Success at eBay

Soon after Skoll came across Pierre Omidyar and his startup, an online auction site. The founder hired Skoll to write a business plan and with this Skoll became the first employee of the company when it was officially born as a company in 1995. In fact, it was also Skoll's home in Palo Alto that served as the company's headquarters during the initial years, as eBay did not even have a real street address. With Omidyar inviting him to become eBay's first President, Skoll quit his job with Knight-Ridder in 1996 and began to work fulltime at eBay. While eBay was already on the path to a profit-making venture by the time Skoll joined the company, it was he who charted the script of eBay's spectacular rise to the foremost auction-cum-marketplace on the internet.

Skoll continued to hold the office of the President of the company till January 1998 when a replacement was found in Meg Whitman. He in turn took on the role of the Vice President, Strategic Planning and Analysis till health issues compelled him to retire from full-time employment at eBay.

Skoll however continues to retain a stake in eBay. And though it is now less than 8 per cent, even then those personal stock holdings were estimated to be worth around 3.7 billion USD in 2005. This is a far cry from the time when the size of Skoll's stake in the company was second only to Omidyar, before he cashed out a part of it which in turn bumped up Skoll's net worth by at least 2 billion USD. In 2007, Skoll formally became a U.S. citizen.

Giving Back to the Community

In recent years, Skoll has been content in the role of philanthropist and film producer, using his resources to bring about positive changes in the world. One way he does this through production of issue-based films under his production banner, 'Participant Media' that was launched in 2004. Since then, it has co-produced more than sixty movies which seek to bring about betterment of less privileged sections of world. Among the most famous productions of the company are the multiple Academy Award winner 'The

Help' as well as the surprise hit, 'The Best Exotic Marigold Hotel'. The documentary title 'Citizenfour' about Edward Snowden is another offering from Participant which won an Academy Award for best feature documentary in 2015.

In April 2015 after then CEO of the company Jim Berk left, Skoll took on the role of interim CEO. With the arrival of a new CEO, David Linde, in October 2015 at Participant, Skoll turned his attention to a new cable channel 'Pivot TV', which is geared towards millennials. In 2013, he reportedly agreed to invest around 200 million USD into the channel.

However the chief vehicle for Skoll's philanthropic initiatives is the Skoll Foundation which he founded as far backs as 2001. With more than 50 million USD in assets, the Foundation supports young social entrepreneurs who are looking for different ways to raise standards of education, healthcare and access to jobs in some of the least developed parts of the planet.

□

23
Jerry Yang

An American internet billionaire of Taiwanese origin, Jerry Yang is most famous as the founder of the Yahoo! navigational guide as well as co-founder and former CEO of Yahoo Inc. After Yahoo, Yang started venture capital firm titled 'AME Cloud Ventures' which has since 2012 invested in more than 50 startups. In 1999, Yang was named to the MIT Technology Review "TR100" as one of the top 100 innovators in the world under the age of 35. With his Yahoo stake as well as investment in Chinese online retail giant, Alibaba, Yang enjoys a net worth of 1.89 billion USD as on June 2016.

Early Years

Born as Jerry Chih-Yuan Yang on 6th November 1968 in Taipei, Taiwan, the future internet mogul lost his father when only two years old. A few years later his mother immigrated with ten year old Jerry and his younger brother to the U.S. In an interesting anecdote, Yang later revealed that though his mother was an English teacher, at the time of their arrival in the United States, he himself knew only one word in the language, "shoes".

However being the brilliant boy he was, Jerry soon caught up with his peers and in the period of just three years, was fluent in English. He went on to study at the Sierramont

Middle School and Piedmont Hills High School, after which he earned a B.S. and M.S. in electrical engineering from Stanford. Yang even started a doctoral program at Stanford but opted out midway.

Birth of Yahoo!

While still in Stanford, Yang met a fellow student of the masters program, David Filo. The two hit off amidst a common interest in computers and internet which led to the launch of a website titled, "Jerry and Dave's Guide to the World Wide Web", in February 1994. This initially consisted of a directory of other websites that provided a wide variety of products and services.

But as it became increasingly popular over the internet, the duo changed the name to a much more manageable 'Yahoo!'. By the fall of 1994, it had received around 100,000 unique visitors. In April 1995, Yahoo! received a 2 million USD investment from Sequoia Capital and in this way it was incorporated as Yahoo Inc. Tim Koogle was hired as CEO of the company while both Yang and Filo received the appointment of "Chief Yahoo".

As a mark of its increasing popularity, Yahoo attracted a second round funding in the fall of 1995, this time from Reuters and Softbank. In April 1996, it finally went public though at the time it had just 49 employees.

Wavering Fortunes

However the dot com bubble bust in the mid-2000s, meant tough times for Yahoo! too. Koogle was criticized for lack of foresight in protecting the company and was replaced by Terry Semel. Semel's tenure as CEO in turn was marked by the meteoric rise of Google and the inability of Yahoo! to handle the competition. Semel was thus fired in 2007 upon which Yang was appointed as interim CEO.

Even Yang's tenure was not free from trouble for Yahoo! During this time, the stock prices and revenues remained in a slump and as a result he came under fire from investors. Things worsened for Yang when he rejected a takeover bid by Microsoft worth 47 billion USD. At the time Yahoo! was struggling to keep up with search giant, Google while Microsoft was looking for a foothold into the web. Industry watchers slammed Yang for rejecting the proposal that stood to benefit both parties. By 2008 the company's shares had dropped to only $14 per share. In response to all this, a new CEO Carol Bartz was brought in while Yang resumed his earlier role of 'Chief Yahoo' and member of Board of Directors. At the time of Yang's resignation from the board Yahoo!'s market capitalization was only 20 billion USD. Around four years later, in 2012, Yang resigned from Yahoo's board as well.

Despite Yahoo's dwindling fortunes in the later part of 2000s, Yang's contribution to the company is undeniable. He played a key role in exploring international ventures as well as chalking out a long-term vision for the company. One proof of this is Yahoo's 1 billion USD investment in Alibaba that Yang pushed forward in 2005. Though he was not yet the CEO, still Yang championed the purchase of a 40 per cent stake in Alibaba for 1 billion USD plus the assets of Yahoo! China, valued at 700 million USD. In 2012 when Yahoo! sold a fraction of its stake in Alibaba, it earned the company a neat 7.6 billion USD. Yahoo! made another 9.4 billion USD in 2014, when Alibaba went public on the New York Stock Exchange. Not surprisingly Eric Jackson, the founder of hedge fund Ironfire Capital, called Yahoo!'s investment in Alibaba "The best investment an American company has ever made in China," and stated, "Jerry deserves enormous credit for that which paid off during its successful September 2014 public offering".

Recent Ventures

Yang's expertise in the internet business and his contribution to the internet media industry has gone beyond

Yahoo. After resigning from the Yahoo's board, he turned his attention on a new generation of tech firms. He founded a venture capital firm called 'AME Cloud Ventures', which has invested in more than 50 data-based startups like Evernote, Wattpad and Tango. Apart from this, Yang continues to serve on the boards of Chinese e-commerce giant Alibaba as well as enterprise software firm 'Workday'.

Personal Life

Yang is married to Akiko Yamazaki, whom he met at Stanford when she was studying for her degree in Industrial Engineering. She is also the director at the Wildlife Conservation Network and the couple lives in Los Altos Hill, California.

Yang is a keen collector of Chinese calligraphy artwork besides being a former Chinese calligraphy student himself. His personal collection includes more than 250 works of ancient Chinese calligraphers from the Ming and Qing eras, some of which were exhibited in late 2012 and early 2013, at the San Francisco's Asian Art Museum. Later this selection was also displayed at the Metropolitan Museum of Art in the 2014 exhibition, "Out of Character: Decoding Chinese Calligraphy".

In recent years, Yang has been busy with several philanthropic initiatives as well. He is a trustee at Stanford and in February 2007, gifted 75 million USD from "Jerry Yang and Akiko Yamazaki Environment and Energy Building" to his *alma mater* which includes multidisciplinary research, teaching and lab sections based on sustainable architecture design.

□

24
Jimmy Wales

Whenever one needs to get some quick information online today, the go-to site for many is the Wikipedia. But who are the brains behind this source of easy reference? One is that of American internet entrepreneur Jimmy Wales who with Lawrence Sanger founded Wikipedia as an open source online encyclopaedia. Though the co-founders remain in dispute over who came up with the idea first, there is little doubt about Wales' role in popularizing Wikipedia as well as its spinning off related online offerings like 'Wiktionary' and 'Wikinews'.

Early Life

Born as Jimmy Donal Wales in Huntsville, Alabama, on August 7, 1966, the future internet success received an unconventional primary education. Till the eighth grade, he studied in a one-room school run by his mother and grandmother according to the Montessori method. One of its features was self-directed study to which he would later credit his own bent for innovation and perseverance. Another consequence of this study method was an unusual reading list, which in Wales' case included a whole range of encyclopedias.

Later Wales attended the Randolph preparatory school after which he enrolled at the Auburn University to study for a graduate degree in finances. He continued his academic leanings with a doctoral program in finance at the University of Alabama. However midway he switched over to Indiana University but eventually opted out of college and took up a job in a financial services firm.

Nupedia and Other Efforts

From 1994 to 2000 Wales worked as an options trader in Chicago, making enough money to enable him to give up a salaried job and take his chances as an entrepreneur. He started his own Internet company called 'Bornis' and although it did not turn out to be very successful, it introduced Wales to the world of internet and online ventures. In the meantime, Wales had also become attracted to objectivist philosophy with its reliance on individualism, capitalism and reason. As part of this new-found vocation, he has since 1989 been moderating the online Ayn Rand Philosophy Discussion List.

Partly influenced by objectivism and its associated theory of openness, Wales began thinking of launching a free online encyclopaedia. The result was 'Nupedia'. Launched in 2000, this was an online encyclopaedia to which volunteers with relevant subject matter expertise could contribute articles, provided they were reviewed by editors prior to publication. Equally importantly Nupedia would be licensed as free content, accessible to any Internet user. For Nupedia Wales roped in American academician and advocate of online education, Larry Sanger to act as the editor-in-chief of the site.

However the process of peer review on Nupedia turned out to be highly time-consuming. Sanger then came across the emerging software of wiki and convinced Wales to try out the model for the project on free online encyclopaedia.

Launch of Wikipedia

The new technology of wiki enabled Wales and Sanger

in 2001 to launch a new companion online encyclopaedia, named 'Wikipedia', that anyone could contribute to and also edit. For a brief while, Nupedia and Wikipedia functioned together but soon it became clear that the latter was attracting much more traffic and contribution on the internet. This led to the decline of Nupedia as well as the emergence of dispute between Wales and Sanger, each of who claimed credit for the idea and success of Wikipedia. Finally with the Sanger facing the prospect of losing his pay, he resigned from both organizations in 2002.

Wales on the other hand continued at the helm of affairs. In 2003, in order to oversee the massive growth of Wikipedia, Wales founded the non-profit 'Wikimedia Foundation'. Under its aegis, the wiki model was extended to other sites like Wikinews and Wiktionary. In 2004 the for-profit 'Wikia, Inc' was co-founded by Wales with a former colleague, Angela Beesley.

By 2006 Wikipedia was one of internet's most popular sites and was being published in multiple languages. However it also came under repeated criticism for reasons, ranging from editorial conflicts and unreliable information to being subjected to deliberate vandalism and even practical jokes. The fact that co-founder Sanger continued to revile Wikipedia in public and media did not make things any easier for Wales. In reaction to Wikipedia, Sanger even launched his own online encyclopaedia called 'Citizendium' which did not allow anonymous editing and where every author/editor would have to be identified by his/her real name.

Eventually though Wikipedia proved to be the more resilient of the two and while Citizendium was forced to shut down due to lack of viewership, Wikipedia has emerged as the quickest and most popular source of reference over a variety of subjects on the internet.

Recent Ventures

Jimmy Wales stepped down as the CEO of the

Wikimedia Foundation in 2009 and has since been busy supporting the cause of open access information on the internet. In 2012, he was roped in by the British government to suggest ways of making government-funded research available to taxpayers without any cost. Wales continues to be on the advisory board of several academic centres and research institutions, pushing for greater openness and accessibility of information on the World Wide Web.

□

25

Larry Page

Ever since the internet became accessible to billions of users around the world, it has become the site of many new inventions, each of which has opened up never imagined before possibilities of this resource. One such invention is the Google Search-the most popular web search engine even now, which enables users to glean information from the World Wide Web. And this was invented by computer scientists, Larry Page and Sergey Brin. In fact Page was the foremost contributor of the PageRank-Google's best-known search ranking algorithm. As a result he is counted among the top Internet entrepreneurs of these times.

Early Life

Born as Lawrence Page on March 26, 1973, in East Lansing, Michigan, the future Internet whiz is one of two children to Carl Vincent and Gloria Page. Both his parents were computer engineers themselves—his father was one of the earliest researchers and Ph.D holders in computer science as well as a pioneer in the field of artificial intelligence. Likewise Larry's mother taught computer programming at Lyman Briggs College at Michigan State University. No wonder then Larry was, right from his childhood, hooked to computers. Reminiscing about his childhood later during an interview, Page described how his house "Was usually a mess with computers, science and technology magazines and popular science magazines all over the place". But this was also an environment that nurtured creativity and technological brilliance.

One of the influences of his earliest days was that of music. While growing up, he played saxophone and also studied music composition. Page later mentioned that his musical education may have in some way inspired his obsession with speed in computing as well as impatience with time lag, "In some sense I feel like music training led to the high-speed legacy of Google for me".

However it was computers which truly enchanted Larry all his childhood. He often tinkered with first-generation personal computer at home that had been used by his parents and became the first student in his elementary school to submit an assignment from a word processor. Before long he was taking gadgets apart to see how they worked and then trying to put it back together again. In a later interview, Larry recalled "From a very early age, I also realized I wanted to invent things. So I became really interested in technology and business. Probably from when I was 12, I knew I was going to start a company eventually."

From 1975 to 1979, Larry attended the Okemos Montessori School in Okemos, Michigan after which he went to East Lansing High School. While still in high school, he studied at the Interlochen Center for the Arts as a saxophonist for two summers. After graduating from high school in 1991, he enrolled in the University of Michigan where he earned a Bachelor of Science with honours in computer engineering and followed it up with Master of Science in computer science from Stanford University.

While looking for a research topic during his Ph.D at Stanford University, Page got interested in the mathematical properties of the World Wide Web with special focus on its link structure as a huge graph. His then supervisor, Terry Winograd heartily supported this line of research and encouraged Page to pursue it. It was at this time that Page met Sergey Brin, a fellow Stanford PhD student who in turn became interested in Page's idea and agreed to work on it as a partner. The research project came to be dubbed BackRub and eventually the two wrote a research paper titled, "The Anatomy of a Large-Scale Hypertextual Web Search Engine," which turned out to be one of the most downloaded documents on technology in the contemporary history of internet.

Google Search

The internet at that time was a maze of information. An estimated 10 million documents, along with an untold number of links between them existed on the World Wide Web and looking for any information here with the existing search engines was a cumbersome, time-consuming affair. Supported by Brin, Page invented a new algorithm that would use a different technology to analyze the relevance of the backlinks that connected one Web page to another. This algorithm was titled 'PageRank', after its inventor and the duo then began to explore the further possibilities of this technology especially on how it could be applied to bring order to all the information on the Web. Eventually Page and Brin created a search engine that listed results according to the popularity of the Page, after concluding that the most popular result would often be the most useful.

However logistics posed to be a problem. At that time both Page and Brin were just students and thus could not afford a proper research station with advanced resources. As a result Page turned his dormitory room into a machine laboratory. Then they began collecting spare parts from inexpensive computers to create a machine which they eventually used to connect their own search engine with Stanford's broadband campus network. When no more space was left in Page's room, Brin's dorm room was used as an office and programming centre. Here the two tested their new search engine designs on the Web. Finally in August 1996, their new search engine was made available to internet users. Though this was still part of the Stanford University website, it soon became so popular that its inventors had to bring in additional servers to deal with the increasing use. The search engine was named "Google" after the mathematical term "googol," which refers to the No. 1 followed by 100 zeros.

Founding of the Company

Page and Brin next started collecting funds to found a company which would help them to commercially launch and operate their search engine. Among family, friends and other investors, they managed to collect $1 million and in 1998, Google Inc was finally incorporated. As the main founder of Google, Page became its CEO, while Brin was named Google's co-founder and became the president of the company. Its mission statement from the outset was "To organize the world's information and make it universally accessible and useful".

Continuous Expansion

In August 2004 Google held its initial public offering and turned its makers Page and Brin into billionaires overnight. In the same year, the company moved into its new headquarters in Mountain View, California, an innovative structure, nicknamed the Googleplex and designed by the famous Clive Wilkinson Architects. As of 2007, it was estimated to run more than one million servers in data centres around the world. In 2006, Google purchased the most popular website for user-submitted streaming videos, YouTube, for $1.65 billion in stock.

In August 2015, Page and Brin announced plans to reorganize the interests of Google Inc as a holding company called 'Alphabet Inc'. This restructuring took place on October 2, 2015, and in consequence Google became Alphabet's leading subsidiary, as well as the parent for Google's Internet interests. Once again Page and Brin were appointed to serve as the new company's CEO and president, respectively, but this time with Indian-born Sundar Pichai taking over as Google's top executive office.

Personal Life

In 2007, Page married research scientist, Lucinda Southworth. The gala wedding was held on Necker Island, owned by British entrepreneur Richard Branson. Larry and Lucinda have two children, born in 2009 and 2011. In recent times Page has been in news for acquiring expensive property, one of the first was 9000-sq ft Spanish Colonial Revival architecture house in Palo Alto, California which is in fact listed in the National Register of Historic Places and had been on the market for years with an asking price of 7.95 million US dollars. Again in 2011, Page bought a 193-ft super yacht 'Senses' for a whopping 45 million US dollars. However in 2013 it was reported that Page was suffering from a paralysis of vocal chords caused by an autoimmune condition known as Hashimoto's thyroiditis.

Legacy

Though the search engine Google was the result of teamwork, the invention of PageRank by Larry Page played a significant role in the designing of the search engine. And since its launch in 1996, Google has maintained its position of the world's most popular search engine. Even in 2013 when several more search engines were available to Web users, Google was still getting an average of 5.9 billion searches per day.

Apart from inventing the algorithm PageRank for Google, Page had an important role in the evolution of the search engine. He believed that a search engine's popularity directly depend on the speed of its search result. He insisted that his team of designers and engineers try their best to overcome lag times and save milliseconds, if need be. Apart from an insistence on speed, Page was also particular about keeping the design of Google's home page uncluttered so that it could load search results faster. Little wonder then in 2015, the *Forbes* site on Page's "Powerful People" profile described Google as "The most influential company of the digital era".

Part of Page's legacy also incorporates the management philosophy he ushered in his company and by extension throughout the Silicon Valley. At the beginning of his tenure as Google CEO, Page took a stand against non-engineers supervising engineers due to the former's limited technical knowledge. Eventually, the rest of the industry based in Silicon Valley too adopted the practice of primarily employing engineers in management roles of engineering teams.

Again during his second stint as Google CEO, Page ensured that executives overseeing the most important divisions had greater autonomy than before and also pushed for greater collaboration, communication and unity among the teams. These changes in the management ethics were eventually reflected in the product too as various applications and services from Google went through better consolidation and an aesthetic overhaul. These initiatives went on to make Page a highly respected personality in the global hi-tech industry. At the completion of 2014, *Fortune* magazine named Page its "Businessperson of the Year," declaring him "The world's most daring CEO." Again next year, in October 2015, Page was named number one in *Forbes*' "America's Most Popular Chief Executives", based on a poll by employees.

Finally Page is a regular supporter of alternative and clean energy initiatives. He has substantial investments in plug-in hybrid electric cars, most notably in Tesla Motors. With the help of Google.org—the philanthropic division of the company, Page promotes the adoption of alternative energy technology as well dissemination of socio-economic benefits of advanced intelligent systems. Though today Page is one of the richest individuals in the world, according to *Forbes* his net worth is $35.5 billion as of April 2016—his true contribution and legacy involves all these ways in which internet and technology has served to create the world a better place.

□

26
Liu Quindaong

Popularly known as Richard Liu, Quindaong is the founder of JD.com or Jingdong Mall, one of the leading e-commerce portals in China. He is both the CEO as well as the director of the company and as of March 2016, enjoyed a net worth of 5.9 billion USD, making him one of the richest people in China.

Early Life

Born as Liu Quindaong on 14 February 1974 in Suqian, Jiangsu province, the future e-commerce pioneer grew in a family that was in the business of transporting coal from north China to the southern manufacturing centres of the country.

After completing school, Liu enrolled in the People's University of China to study for a degree in sociology as in those times that particular academic department was reputed for its connection to political elite of the country. In 1996 he graduated with a bachelor's degree and then went on to study for an EMBA from the China Europe International Business School.

Learning on the Job

However, Liu also knew that the degrees alone would not guarantee a good job in the market. And in order to add on to his skills, he started learning computer programming in his spare time, which was rather unusual at that time in China. While still a student he also started freelancing as a coder with the aim of starting his own business. Soon he had saved enough to open his own restaurant but thinking that he lacked the experience to manage a business, he allowed others to take over the role. That turned out to be a bad decision as his staff embezzled money and Liu hurtled towards to bankruptcy within just a few months of opening his restaurant. However the experience gave him valuable lessons in entrepreneurship and later in an interview to *Financial Times* in 2012, he said, "During the two years there, I gradually understood that the restaurant bankruptcy was my fault because I had not established management structures, done oversight or established financial systems and procedures."

After completing his studies, Liu decided to take up a job with Japan Life, a Japanese health product enterprise. Here he served by turns in the roles of the director for computers, the director for business and the logistics supervisor. More importantly he was able to pay off his debts with the monthly paycheck that he got from the job.

Success Second Time Over

Two years later, in June 1998, Liu felt himself ready to launch his own business again. With just 12,000 Yuan, that he had saved from his salaries, he established Jingdong Century Trading, located in the Zhongguancun High-tech Industrial Park in Beijing. His firm was a consumer electronics shop specializing in magneto-optical products. This time he was successful in his enterprise and within a span of just five years, he had opened 12 stores in the chain and taken his earnings to more than 10 million Yuan.

However in 2003, Liu found himself in another challenge—the SARS outbreak in China which compelled people to stay largely indoors. As a result, Liu found his firm suffering from the absence of both the staff and customers and once again Jingdong came close to financial ruin.

But like all great leaders, Liu too saw in this crisis a window of opportunity. Since people in China at the time were reluctant to go out for fear of contacting the SARS virus, they preferred to stay indoors and shop. This gave a major fillip to e-commerce in China and Liu too began rethinking his business model. He deduced, correctly, that even after the epidemic subsided, people would continue with the practice of shopping online once they had experienced first-hand its benefits. Realizing this potential for new opportunity, Liu decided to divert to online business.

In 2004 Liu made his debut in online retail with the launch of the website JD.com which was the abbreviation for Jingdong. By 2005, Liu had shut down all brick-and-mortar stores and become an entirely e-commerce entrepreneur.

Meeting Challenges

Initially the move to the digital world suffered from teething problems. Sales at Jingdong dropped to 30 million Yuan, less than half of what it had made the previous year. Liu however maintained his focus and in the next five years, from 2004 to 2009—the company recorded an average growth rate of more than a whopping 300 per cent.

Yet another challenge that JD.com faced was the competition from leading players in the Chinese online retail market, like Alibaba, which owns major portals like Taobao and Tmall. However under Liu's stewardship, the company got a much needed boost from Tencent, another competitor of Alibaba. In return for a 15 per cent stake in JD, Tencent pumped in around 214.7 million USD in cash into Liu's company. Apart from this, Tencent also handed over to JD.com two of its e-commerce businesses-QQ Wanggou and Paipai—besides a minority stake in Yixun. Industry experts recognized that by acquiring a stake in JD, which had by then emerged as mainland China's second-largest business-to-consumer platform, Tencent would be able to offer Alibaba a strong competition in e-commerce. For JD.com on the other hand, the deal brought in valuable funding with which it was able to go public on NASDAQ in 2014. This not only made history as the third-largest initial public offering in the US that year but with this, JD was able to beat its main rival Alibaba to an IPO.

Sweet Success

JD.com is now counted as among the leading e-commerce businesses in China. According to *Forbes*, Liu enjoys a current net worth around 6 billion USD, making him one of the 100 richest individuals in China. More importantly Liu holds an 84 per cent of voting power under a dual-class share structure in his company, thus giving complete control—through veto power, over all future decisions at JD.com.

Personal Life

Not surprisingly for a man of his wealth and success, Liu's personal life has often found him on the front pages of the Chinese media. His relationships have especially garnered a lot of interest. According to media reports, Liu's first relationship was with a fellow student from his university days, Gong Xiaojing. In fact the company that he founded, Jingdong Mall, was named in a way so as to put Jing—the last character of Gong Xiaojing and Dong last character of his name Liu's surname, Qiangdong-together. Gong however chose a different life, that of a government employee.

Liu's second relationship was with Zhuang Jia, a senior employee at JD.com, in-charge of the purchase and sales of small home appliances. In fact the relationship became public when tweets about the couple's home-grown tomatoes appeared on Chinese microblogging site Weibo, in an incident that came to be dubbed, 'Tomato Gate'. Zhuang left

JD.com shortly after its successful launch of a small home appliances business.

In early 2014, news broke out in the Chinese media about Liu dating internet celebrity Zhang Zetian who is better known among netizens as "Sister Milk Tea", for her photo-holding milk tea posted and followed on Weibo. Apparently the two had started dating in New York City where Zhang had gone as an exchange student at Barnard College, an affiliate of Columbia University. On August 8, 2015, Liu Qiangdong and Zhang Zetian registered for marriage in Beijing after which they held a lavish wedding ceremony in Sydney, Australia on October 1, 2015.

Currently, Liu has been busy with giving JD.com a global presence for which he has been courting foreign brands. In fact in July 2015 the company announced—it reached a deal with pop sensation singer Taylor Swift to promote the sale of apparel directed at the Chinese market. In January 2016 JD.com also invested $50 million in shopping startup 'Wish' and seems poised to ink many more interesting deals to fulfil its ambitious business plans.

□

27

Luke Nosek

Luke Nosek is an American entrepreneur of Polish origin who is best known for co-founding PayPal, a popular online payment portal. Since its acquisition by eBay in 2002 for 1.5 billion USD, Nosek has been busy as an astute, venture capitalist, investing in several startups as well looking into the affairs of high tech companies like SpaceX and ResearchGate where he is part of the Board.

Early Life

Nosek was born in Poland in 1975. Eventually he migrated with his family to the United States where after school, he worked hard to earn B.S. degree in Computer Engineering from the University of Illinois at Urbana-Champaign. While still in college, he co-founded SponsorNet New Media, Inc., along with fellow Illinois students Max Levchin and Scott Banister in the summer of 1995. After graduating from college, Nosek worked for some time in Netscape Communications Corporation.

Success with PayPal

However Nosek's real interest lay in entrepreneurship and in 1998, he became part of a group of tech experts that included Peter Thiel, Max Levchin, Elon Musk, and Ken Howery. This group went on to launch an online system of electronic payments known as PayPal. While the basic idea was to cater to the burgeoning industry of e-commerce, the group also had the vision of designing a system that would replace, what Nosek later termed 'The antique technology' of paper money.

PayPal was designed to operate as what in financial circles is known as acquirer-charging a fee to facilitate payment processing for online vendors, auction sites and other commercial users on the internet. Upon its inception, Nosek served as vice-president of marketing and strategy in PayPal where his primary contribution was the creation of the company's "instant transfer", product. However in the early years, PayPal often faced challenges in the form of banking and Visa Card regulations. Despite certain initial hiccups, PayPal soon became popular enough to be recognized as one of the world's largest Internet payment companies. Its success prompted eBay to acquire it in 2002 for 1.5 billion USD.

In the middle of 2015, eBay decided to spin-off PayPal into an independent company. After this it went through a second IPO on July 20, 2015, when it was accorded a valuation of 46.6 billion USD.

The PayPal Group

PayPal proved not only a hit in the e-commerce sector but impacted the tech world in far-reaching ways. In fact several founders and employees of PayPal eventually launched their own startups that developed into some of the key technology companies of the Silicon Valley in the past decade. Elon Musk for instance founded the rocket making company SpaceX and co-founded eco-friendly auto makers, Tesla Motors. Reid Hoffman on the other hand co-founded LinkedIn, a network connecting professionals while David Sacks co-founded Yammer, a social networking service used within organizations for private communication. Max Levchin would go on to launch Yelp, the 'online urban guide' while Thiel would become famous as the first outside investor in the social networking giant, Facebook. This trend among the PayPal co-founders earned them the nickname of 'the PayPal Mafia'.

Recent Initiatives

After the takeover of PayPal by eBay in 2002, Nosek decided to enter the venture capital market. In early 2005 Founders Fund was launched by Nosek and some members of the PayPal founding team, namely Peter Thiel and Ken Howery while Sean Parker, an early employee of Napster and ex-president of Facebook, joined in 2006.

Based in San Francisco, Founders Fund was created to provide investments in companies building revolutionary technologies. The firm invests at all stages across a wide variety of sectors, ranging from fundamental ones like energy, health and consumer internet to highly specialized like aerospace, advanced computing and even artificial intelligence. In January 2005, the firm raised its first fund of 50 million USD from individual entrepreneurs and angel investors.

As part of Founders Fund, Nosek's biggest investments have been in companies launched by his former PayPal partners. In fact, he was the first institutional backer in SpaceX, an aerospace company founded by Elon Musk. The initial investment of Nosek's fund into SpaceX was 20 million USD, which with subsequent investments too, Founders Fund's holding in the company to a substantial 500 million USD—an initiative Nosek justified as that the progress of the company was "Critical to the human race."

Nosek was again the earliest investor of Geni, a tech company founded by former PayPal COO David Sacks. Later Geni spun out Yammer which in turn was acquired by Microsoft in June 2012 for 1.2 billion USD.

Yet another high tech firm that Founders Fund seeded at the earliest stages to the tune of 15 million USD was Deep

Mind Technologies, the British artificial intelligence company which was later taken over by Google for £240 million. Other companies that are part of the Founders Fund portfolio include Halcyon Molecular and Practice Fusion. As of 2014, Founders Fund had more than $2 billion in aggregate capital under management.

Achievements

Nosek's contribution in the creation of PayPal and later Founders Fund led him to feature at the 92nd position in the 2013 *Midas* list, which is released by *Forbes* to rank the world's smartest investors in the technology sector. However it is not just work that Nosek keeps himself busy with. One of the major passions is Yoga—he not only practices daily meditation but also finds time to get away to several retreats a year in order to further his study of this ancient philosophy. □

28
Mark Pincus

With the rise of social networking sites, social gaming too has become all the rage among netizens. And the man who seems to have played a pioneering role in this field is Mark Pincus, co-founder and former CEO of Zynga which is known for immensely popular online social games like Cityville and Farmville. He continues to hold the position of the Chairman at Zynga and his net worth is estimated to be around 1.16 billion USD as of April, 2016 according to Forbes.com.

Early Life

Born Mark Jonathan Pincus on February 13, 1966, the future online gaming mogul was raised in an upper middle class Jewish family in Chicago along with two sisters, Laura Pincus Hartman and Susan Pincus Sherman. His father was a public relations official while his mother was an architect.

Right from kindergarten through high school Pincus studied at the Francis W. Parker School from where he graduated in 1984. Being a brilliant student and with the support of his parents, he then enrolled in the Wharton School of the University of Pennsylvania where he earned his Bachelor of Science degree in Economics. With such a degree Pincus had no trouble finding work in the financial services industry. His first major employer was Lazard Freres & Co.

where he remained for two years and then moved to Hong Kong as the Vice President for Asian Capital Partners for another couple of years.

Pincus next decided to upgrade his skills and thus joined Harvard Business School to study for an MBA. After his graduation in 1993, he was made the manager of corporate development at Tele-Communications, Inc., which is presently known as AT&T Cable. Soon after Pincus moved to Washington, D.C where he joined Columbia Capital as Vice President.

At Columbia Capital, Pincus was in-charge of investments in new media and software startups. And this gave him the exposure to the world of online ventures. He was enthused enough to launch a series of startups, beginning with Freeloader, Inc in 1995, a web-based push technology service. With his very first venture, Pincus tasted success as Freeloader, was lapped up just seven months later for 38 million USD by Individual, Inc.

Next followed Support.com that Pincus launched in August 1997 as a provider of service and support automation software. This proved to be more successful than Pincus' previous venture and even went public in July 2000. Two years later, it underwent a major rebranding with its name being changed from Support.com to SupportSoft, Inc. In 2003, Pincus launched his third online enterprise that was an early version of a social network, named Tribe.net.

Success with Zynga

In 2007, a company named, Zynga Inc was launched by Pincus and his team that included Justin Waldron, Eric Schiermeyer, Michael Luxton and Steve Schoettler. According to an interesting anecdote, Pincus named the company after his late pet dog. Zynga would go on to create highly popular online social games like Words with Friends, Castleville, Cityville, Farmville, Scramble with Friends Zynga, Poker and others that could be played on various social networks including Facebook, as well as on mobile devices including the Android, iPhone and iPad. The Zynga network not only includes games that are developed by in-house designers but also those created by third-party developers. Zynga claims to be the largest social game network on the web with a current active user base of 123 million monthly active users across its network of games.

As Zynga's success graph rose higher, Pincus and his team decided to take the company public. On December 16, 2011 Zynga made its debut in the New York Stock Exchange in what turned out to be the largest initial public offering in the technology sector since the appearance of Google in 2004. It earned 1 billion USD for the company which was set at a 7 billion USD valuation.

However the next eighteen months proved to be difficult. The company's performance in the public markets turned out to be disheartening and it retaliated by firing workers. Additionally it faced lawsuits by competitors and investors—all of which took its share value down by as much as 65 per cent.

In April 2012, Pincus sold off about 16.5 million Zynga's shares in a move that was widely criticized in the industry as well as the media, especially since while employees were forced to hold on to their shares during this period of steep slide of the company's stocks.

In June 2013, following hardened opposition to his leadership, Pincus stepped down from the position of the CEO in favour of Microsoft executive, Dan Mattrick. However in April 2015, Pincus was brought back as the Chief Executive only to give way again a year later to Frank Gibeau. Pincus though continues to serve as Chairman of the Board at Zynga Inc.

Apart from being a serial startup entrepreneur, Pincus was also an early investor in various online ventures like Napster, Twitter and Facebook. Apparently he drew on his earlier work experience to spot startups with potential and wisely invested in them.

Personal Life

Pincus is married to Alison who is an internet entrepreneur as well and has co-founded 'One Kings Lane', a flash sales site for home goods. The couple has three children and live in San Francisco. In recent times, Pincus has been in the media for his lavish lifestyle. He owns luxury homes in San Francisco and Washington DC and has a private jet too among his possessions.

At the same time though, Pincus has launched several non-profit initiatives through the Zynga.org, the philanthropic arm of Zynga Inc., in 2011, the company announced that the entire proceeds garnered by the sale of virtual goods from more than seven of its games would be handed over to Save the Children Earthquake Emergency Fund of Japan. Again during the 2012 holiday season, Zynga.org partnered with Toys for Tots to raise 745,000 USD, in what turned out to be its largest charitable campaign unrelated to disaster relief.

□

29
Mark Zuckerberg

Feted as one of the youngest billionaires on the planet, Mark Zuckerberg is the co-founder and current CEO of the immensely popular social networking site 'Facebook'. In 2012, at 28 he added another feather to his cap by becoming the youngest CEO of a *Fortune* 1000 company to go public. As of June 2016, Zuckerberg enjoyed a net worth of $49 billion USD according to *Forbes*, making him its richest entrepreneur under 50 as well the fourth wealthiest billionaire person in the world in 2015.

Early Life

Born as Mark Elliot Zuckerberg on May 14, 1984, in White Plains, New York, to Edward and Karen Zuckerberg, the brains behind Facebook, was one of couple's four children. Mark's father ran a successful dental practice while his mother was a psychiatrist. The rest of the family was made up of three sisters named Randi, Donna and Arielle.

Mark's interest in computers was evident from an early age and when only twelve, he used Atari BASIC to create his first program—a messaging service which was in fact used by his family members to communicate within the house and even by his father in his dental office. Additionally Mark enjoyed designing computer games with his friends. His parents did their best to nurture Mark's prodigious gift—

hiring a private tutor to teach him programming, signing him up Mark in a college where he took graduate courses and enrolling him in an exclusive preparatory school-Phillips Exeter Academy in New Hampshire. Even before graduating high school, Mark created a music software that he named 'Synapse' which went on to become the model of the later Pandora. The software even impressed tech giants like AOL and Microsoft who were not only keen on buying Synapse but also ready to offer him a job straightaway. Yet to complete high school, Mark wisely declined the offer.

After joining Harvard in 2002, Mark found even more opportunities to create youth-oriented programs and softwares and soon developed a reputation as a tech whiz. Among his earliest creations was 'CourseMatch' which enabled students to choose courses based on other's selections as well as 'Facemash' that allowed users to compare and rate photos of attractive looking students. The latter was banned by the college administration but not before it proved to be a raging hit on the campus. Based on his reputation as an innovative developer, Zuckerberg was sought out by a group of Harvard students to design a dating software for privileged students to be called Harvard Connection. This set Zuckerberg thinking on the lines of a social networking program and soon he began giving expression to his own vision.

Soon Zuckerberg roped in a few of his friends, namely Dustin Moskovitz, Chris Hughes and Eduardo Saverin, for his project. The final result was a site that allowed users to create their own profiles, upload photos and communicate with other users. Named Facebook, it went live on February 4, 2004 and till June that year, Zuckerberg continued to run it out of his dorm room at Harvard from where it quickly spread to other schools which had social contacts with Harvard like Stanford, Dartmouth, Columbia, New York University, Cornell, Penn, Brown and Yale. The burgeoning volume of traffic on Facebook made Zuckerberg realize that he would have to develop it into a proper company and devote himself to it full-time. Thus after his sophomore year, Zuckerberg moved to Palo Alto in California.

A Phenomenal Success

Facebook expanded by leaps and bounds and by the end of 2004, it had 1 million users. Next year venture capital giant Accel Partners agreed to invest 12.7 million USD into the network, thus boosting its prospects a great deal. This enabled Zuckerberg expand Facebook from the confines of Ivy League institutions to other schools, colleges and even international institutions, thus bringing the site's membership to a whopping 5.5 million users by December 2005. Soon enough other companies attracted by Facebook's surging popularity among the youth wanted to advertize on the site. Zuckerberg consistently refused buyout attempts from as big companies as Yahoo and MTV Networks.

Then came the first of its legal problems. Zuckerberg was accused by makers of Harvard Connection of stealing their idea and asked pay for their business losses. Though both parties initially reached a settlement of 65 million USD, legal bickering over the issue continued till 2011. Also around this time Zuckerberg fell out with his earlier partner Eduardo Saverin who accused Facebook of diluting his stock in the company. Once again, Facebook reached an out of court settlement, according to which Saverin would receive around 5 per cent stake as well as the status of a co-founder on Facebook's website but in turn, he would have to sign a non-disclosure contract.

In May 2012 Zuckerberg finally emerged triumphant when Facebook went global and got the biggest IPO in history, raising 16 billion USD in the process. Not surprisingly the next year, Facebook made its debut in the list of the *Fortune* 500 companies which in turn made Zuckerberg, then aged only 28, the youngest CEO on the list. Today Zuckerberg continues to hold more than a quarter of stocks of Facebook and controls 57 per cent of the voting shares in the company.

In his personal life too, Zuckerberg has found success. On May 19, 2012, he got married to long-time girlfriend Priscilla Chan who graduated from medical school the same year. The couple welcomed their first child, a daughter named Max on November 2015.

Philanthropic Interest

In recent years Zuckerberg has drawn increasingly closer to philanthropic initiatives and on December 1, 2015, Zuckerberg and his wife announced they would give 99 per cent of their Facebook shares to charity. Zuckerberg's success and impact on the tech world can be gauged from the fact that since 2010, he has consistently figured on the *'Time'* magazine list of the 100 wealthiest and most influential people in the world.

□

30

Matt Mullenweg

For bloggers across the world, WordPress is one of the most sought after content management systems because of its user-friendly interface as well as wide range of creative tools. And the main person behind this is Matt Mullenweg, an American web developer and internet entrepreneur who is based in San Francisco. In 2004, he along with his team developed the definitive version of the free and open source web software 'WordPress', which is now managed by The WordPress Foundation. This not only helped Mullenweg to win the third rank on Business Insider's 2011 list of 30 Founders under 30 but had a larger impact on the tech world by making WordPress the driving force behind many new startups.

Early Life

Born as Matthew Charles Mullenweg on January 11, 1984 in Houston, Texas, the future blogging innovator was surprisingly interested more in the arts rather than computers during his school years. In fact Mullenweg attended the High School for the Performing and Visual Arts in order to study jazz saxophone, among other things.

Next Mullen enrolled in the University of Houston, with the aim of majoring in Political Science. It was during his college years, that he really discovered computers and got hooked to software and coding. Once while jazzing up his photos from a trip, he came across b2/cafelog that had been created by Michel Valdrighi in 2001. Mullenweg kept tinkering with it for the next few years and in May 2003, with Mike Little he forked b2 and created the rudimentary form of WordPress.

WordPress Takes Shape

In 2004, Mullenweg decided to quit college in order to take up a job at CNET Networks even as he continued to work on WordPress. The same year Plugins were introduced with Version 1.2 (Mingus) of the blogging software. By 2005, Mullenweg realized that WordPress would need all his attention and thus he quit CNET. The same year, Version 1.5 (Strayhorn) got its theme system and static pages which in turn was followed by persistent caching, a new user role system, and a new backend UI in Version 2.0 (Duke).

Yet another significant addition to WordPress in 2005 was Akismet, a tool to counter comment and trackback spam. Finally in December 2005, Mullenweg founded the company Automattic in order to run the businesses of WordPress.com and Akismet.

Years of Growth

In 2006, Mullenweg managed to recruit one of the executives of Yahoo, Toni Schneider, in the role of CEO at Automattic. The same year saw the company able to raise 1.1 million USD in funding from investors such as CNET, True Ventures, Radar Partners, and a few other major tech companies of the time. In 2008 the company embarked on another round of funding and managed to raise 29.5 million USD in the month of January. Around this time, WordPress began to attract the attention of the tech industry which began to realize the true potential of what the company had to offer. Such was the immense popularity of WordPress across the web that it not only raced ahead of Google's Blogger service, but even left behind SixApart, till then its closest competitor.

By 2012, it was estimated that WordPress had powered nearly 70 million different websites across the internet which in turn had helped it to earn a staggering 45 million USD of revenue in a single year.

Two years later, Automattic announced another round of funding and was able to garner 160 million USD which put its valuation to a whopping 1.16 billion USD. Mullenweg explained the frequent rounds of funding initiated by Automattic, with their aim remaining a strong independent company. He reasoned that the company wished to work with all the internet giants like Google, Twitter, Facebook and so on. However if it agreed to be acquired by any one of them, it would not be able to work with everyone. The latest round of financing left little doubt about the success of Automattic and WordPress as they were known to power more than 20 per cent of the Web. Mullenweg himself was believed to have a net worth of $400 million from his company Automattic, his work with CNET as well as his blogging software.

Philanthropic Initiatives

In recent years, Mullenweg has become interested in several philanthropic causes across the world. He is deeply associated with the non-profit organization named 'Charity: Water' and is a member of their 'The Well' initiative. As part of this, he visited Ethiopia in February 2012 in order to fund efforts to provide clean and safe drinking water there as well as in other developing countries.

Closer home Mullenweg was a major supporter of The Bay Lights project, an artistic installation of illumination sculpture along San Francisco's Bay Area. Mullenweg was not only the first donor of this project but later he funded its finishing touches as well with an additional 1.5 million USD donation. Other non-profit organizations that Mullenweg supports include Electronic Frontier Foundation, Archive.org, Free Software Foundation, the Innocence Project as well as Long Now.

The impact of Mullenweg's work and WordPress has been tremendous on the World Wide Web. Since it allows anyone to create their own website, it has been estimated that around 20 per cent of all websites that exist, owe their designing to this software. Used on millions of sites, WordPress has undeniably emerged as the largest and most popular self-hosted blogging tool in the world today.

□

31

Mike Krieger

Mike Krieger is an internet entrepreneur of Brazilian origin who with Kevin Systrom, co-founded the highly popular photofiltering and sharing app 'Instagram' which had been used by 400 million people worldwide as of November 2015.

Early Life

Born on March 4, 1986 as Michel Krieger in São Paulo, Brazil, the future co-founder of Instagram grew up in various places since his father worked at Seagram, the Canada-based multinational beverages group. As a result, Krieger's family by turns lived in Portugal, Argentina and the United States. This kind of international exposure, helped Krieger to become multilingual and appreciate a cosmopolitan way of life.

The other influence on young Krieger was computers. His father brought home a computer when Krieger was just six years old. But as soon as he saw the machine, he was hooked and soon he learnt to write software and build his own hardware too. In 2004, Krieger moved to California to attend Stanford University where he specialized in a paper on human-computer interaction which would eventually play a significant role in his understanding of the demands of users of photo apps and accordingly his designing of Instagram.

Yet another way, Krieger's time at Stanford impacted his future was, by bringing him in contact with another student called Kevin Systrom during a course on symbolic systems that both had signed up for.

After graduating from Stanford, Krieger started working with Meebo as a user experience designer and engineer. Meebo was a browser-based instant messaging platform and at the time it was thought to be one of the smartest Silicon Valley startups.

In 2010, once again Krieger came across Systrom—this time when they kept running into each other at Coffee Bar, a popular haunt of the Silicon Valley techies in the Potrero Hill district of San Francisco. Systrom confided in Krieger about his plans for building a check-in and photos service to be named Burbn which was to be something like Foursquare, at that time a popular location-based social networking app.

Instant Success with Instagram

Soon Krieger became interested in Systrom's ideas but what finally emerged was rather different from what the original vision had been—instead of an app which indicated the location of users, the duo now began focusing on one that would simply display pictures, with various filters and make it possible for users to share with their friends and contacts. In this way Instagram was launched in October 2010, initially in Apple's App Store. In the span of next eighteen months, it had been downloaded by at least 30 million iPhone users. In fact within just a year of its launch, Instagram had already notched up its monthly active users from 4 million to 30 million. During the same time frame, its staff strength also rose from four people working for the company to a dozen employees. In recent times the designers have come up with a web version as they have realized its importance in long-term sustenance of the product.

Acquisition by Facebook

In 2010, Instagram first attracted seed funding from Andreessen-Horowitz and Baseline Ventures. Almost a year later, in early 2011 the company completed 7 million USD Series A funding from Benchmark Capital and a few angel investors, like Adam D'Angelo, Jack Dorsey, and Chris Sacca. At the time, Instagram was valued at around 20 million USD. However in 2012 it managed to raise a whopping $50 million in its third round of funding last in a Series B venture, led by Sequoia Capital. Not surprisingly the company too was valued at a staggering a 500 million USD. Soon though the company announced its acquisition by Facebook for a whopping sum of 1 billion USD, of which $300 million would be in cash and the rest in Facebook stock.

Fame and Wealth

With Krieger owning around 10 per cent of Instagram, the acquisition by Facebook made him richer by at least 100 million USD. Interestingly Systrom himself had met Facebook founder Zuckerberg once during the early days of the social networking site. Apparently, Zuckerberg had then invited Systrom to come on board Facebook but the latter had declined saying that he wanted to finish college first. And now, once again destiny had brought them together, with Zuckerberg's Facebook bidding for Systrom's company.

Krieger's role in the designing and running of Instagram has been mainly technical. For the first 3 years it was public, he made the updates for the app and continues to leads its engineering team till today.

Rising Popularity

In 2012, Instagram introduced an Android version of the app which, within a mere 12 hours on the market, was downloaded 1 million times. Even now the basic service on Instagram remains free. "We believe that the core of our product will always be free," the company claims on its website but goes on to add that, "There will be opportunities for consumers to buy extra add-ons like special filters, etc."

Despite being acquired by Facebook, Instagram runs as an independent unit. Presently it has more than 250 employees on its payroll. However in recent years there have been certain signs of influence of the social network, for instance an online advertising system was introduced in 2013, that allows marketers to take note of photographic ads inside the feeds of Instagram users. Because of such measures, it has been estimated by some experts that Instagram could generate between 1.2 and 2 billion USD in revenues in 2016.

Other Interests

Despite all the fame and success, Mike Krieger remains a soft-spoken person, happy to stay behind the camera rather than in front. In fact at Instagram he feed feature pictures of his Burmese mountain dog, Juno as well as stills of beautiful landscapes and skies rather than his own pictures. He is married to Kaitlyn Trigger and both are ardent philanthropists. In April 2015, Krieger announced a partnership with charity evaluator GiveWell, announcing that over the next two years, he would donate 750,000 USD to support charitable initiatives, identified through the Open Philanthropy Project Process.

□

32

Murray and Jack Hidary

Murray and Jack Hidary are brothers who have collaborated in finance and technology-based enterprises. The best known of these is the IT information portal, 'Earthweb' which later came to be known as Dice Inc. While Murray is an artist and musician as well, Jack is an ardent advocate of clean energy as well as an expert in transportation technology and policy.

Early Life

Jack and Murray Hidary grew up in a Jewish family of four brothers and one sister. Their ancestors were of Syrian origin who came to the US as immigrants and settled in Ellis Island. The Hidary brothers grew up in Brooklyn where they absorbed its cosmopolitan influences and picked up the first of their entrepreneurial skills.

Later Jack studied philosophy and neuroscience at Columbia University and was even awarded a Stanley Fellowship in Clinical Neuroscience at the National Institutes of Health. Murray on the other hand would go in a different direction to major in Music and Composition at New York University.

Success with EarthWeb

However the two came together in 1995 to start their

first successful venture known as EarthWeb. At the time this was one of the earliest internet consulting companies in the business. A couple of years later, the Hidary brothers convinced French-born author and internet activist Tristan Louis to join the company. Louis' entry brought about a definite shift in the direction of the company which soon emerged as a successful information portal of the information technology and computer business.

Louis was also the brains behind developer.com which enabled EarthWeb to go public in a spectacular manner on 11 November 1998. The company's initial public offering on that day closed at 48.69 USD per share, which marked a staggering rise of 247.8 per cent from its opening price of 14 USD. In fact at that point of time, EarthWeb's first-day return was among the highest in the history of NASDAQ.

In 1999 EarthWeb acquired dice.com which was then the most popular career website aimed at technology and engineering professionals. This was followed by the company going private and being renamed to Dice Inc. Five years later it was sold to the private equity firms Quadrangle and General Atlantic Partners for approximately 200 million USD.

Later Ventures

However it was not the end of collaboration for Jack and Murray Hidary who got together in 2001 to found yet another company, named 'Vista Research'. This was an independent financial research company with institutional investors as its main clients. For the purpose, Vista drew on the expertise of a vast range of professionals from technology, media and telecommunications sectors to those in energy, aerospace and healthcare. In 2005, Vista Research was taken over by the division of McGraw-Hill that belonged to Standard & Poor after which it was sold to Guidepoint Global, a global consulting and research firm in 2009.

Towards the middle of 2000s, the crisis in the publishing industry prompted Murray Hidary to think of a way of going beyond the book and enable writers to directly connect with their readers. The result was 'iAmplify', yet another online venture founded with Jack in 2005. This was designed as Web-based content publisher and syndication network for a broad range of professionals who could use simple tools on the site to distribute their media. Users at this site varied from big corporations to individual freelancers. iAmplify has since established partnerships with big names like Bloomberg, Condé Nast's Golf Digest, Yoga Journal, Marianne Williamson, David Allen, and Eckhart Tolle.

Other Interests

Jack Hidary has since devoted his resources and expertise to the propagation of renewable energy. He is also a well-regarded consultant in transportation technology and policy. Due to his expertise in all these areas, he sits on board of trustees of XPRIZE, a non-profit organization that designs and manages public competitions aimed at technological development that improves quality of life for all. As part of this role and in order to popularize the use of clean energy, Jack Hidary co-founded the Auto X Prize, to be given to leading developers of highly fuel-efficient vehicles. Currently he is the Chairman for Samba Energy, a provider of software and services that helps commercial buildings bring about energy efficiency and other clients use clean energy.

After iAmplify, Murray Hidary launched a few more online initiatives like Primary Insight, eBility and Giveme. Like Vista Research, Primary Insight was again a provider of experts across multiple industries that had some of the world's largest hedge funds and institutional investors as clients. eBility on the other hand was a cloud-based SaaS platform that enabled professionals from various industries manage and bill their time. Giveme on the other hand is a private app that uses location to share photos and images among a close network of contacts.

Apart from being a digital entrepreneur, Murray is an accomplished musician who has several original compositions to his credit—some of these are titled, 'Motion', 'Spinning Still', 'In Solitude' and 'As You Like'. He is also the creator of Mind Travel which features live piano compositions along with visual art installations.

Murray Hidary is also a keen photographer and his interest in the medium goes back to a cross-country road trip that he took as seventeen-year old. His works have been exhibited in reputed museums—like the Guggenheim Museum in New York and the San Diego Art Institute—and galleries around the world, both as part of group shows and solo displays. They also figure in many expensive private collections. His multifarious talents are also evident in the sporting arena as he has trained for and completed three marathons, New York City and London in 2007 as well as New York City in 2008 too.

☐

33
Nick Denton

British internet mogul Nick Denton is best known as the founder of Gawker Media, the company that own a network of highly popular blogs. In 2010, Denton's blogs attracted as many as 17.5 million U.S. visitors per month, making the company America's 45th most popular online destination during that time.

Early Life

Nick Denton was born on 24 August 1966 at Hampstead in London. His father Geoffrey Denton was an economics professor while his mother Maria was a survivor of the 1956 Soviet invasion of Hungary. After arriving in England, she started studying economics first at London University, then at Southampton, which is reportedly how she met Geoffrey Denton. A woman of wide ranging intellect, she spoke apart from her native Hungarian, Russian, German and Latin as well as English.

As the son of such accomplished parents Nick, not surprisingly, got the best of education. After graduating from University College School, he attended University College, Oxford where he studied Philosophy, Politics and Economics. During this time he also edited 'Isis', the university's magazine, that had in the past featured writings by famous authors as Graham Greene and Evelyn Waugh. Continuing his literary leanings, Denton took up a job with the '*Financial Times*' after his graduation and co-wrote a book titled *All That Glitters* which dealt with the collapse of Barings Bank.

Initial Online Ventures

Denton's first online venture was a networking forum nick named 'First Tuesday' that he co-founded with Adam Gold, Julie Meyer, Mark Davies, and John Browning. As suggested by its moniker, the group would meet each first Tuesday of the month to discuss technology startups, investors and related service providers.

After this Denton co-founded a media-monitoring service named 'Moreover Technologies', with two of his former mates from UCS, David Galbraith and Angus Bankes.

Soon after Denton moved to the US since he believed the West Coast to be much more amenable to internet ventures. Though both First Tuesday and Moreover Technologies were moderate successes, it took him some time to fit into the West Coast Culture which could not completely appreciate his European cosmopolitanism.

Year 2001 proved to be a difficult year – not only because the World Trade Center terrorist attacks sent shock waves across the country but more because of a personal reason. Denton found out that his mother – to whom he had always been close – was dying from cancer. In order to provide himself with a distraction, Denton moved to New York in the summer of 2002.

Success with Gawker

After settling down in New York, Denton got the idea of starting a blog on topics that would interest – like him – any new arrival to the city. This resulted in the birth of a blog named 'Gawker' which originally carried listings on music, nightlife, restaurants and other hangouts in the Big Apple. Soon though he came across another blog called 'Capital Influx', which was run by a young financial analyst named Elizabeth Spiers. Inspired by this, Denton modified the tone of his own to a new gossipy and sardonic style which offered a witty critique of the pretentious people and institutions around him. Even then Gawker and its allied blogs like proved to be only moderate successes.

In March 2006, Denton hit upon the idea to integrate the Gawker Stalker feature–which allowed users to post celebrity sightings online—on his main blog with Google Maps. Practically overnight the readership of Gawker expanded and ever since it has been a favourite destination for getting all the cool, unconventional gossip on every topic under the sun.

Apart from Gawker.com that makes up its flagship property, Gawker Media includes other blogs such as 'Jezebel' on women's issues, 'Gizmodo' on gadgets, 'Jalopnik' on cars, 'Lifehacker' that offers some valuable practical advice and 'Kotaku', a gaming site. Apart from these there is a science-fiction blog named 'i09' and even one on adult content named, 'Fleshbot'.

Though Denton has come under repeated criticism from mainstream media about the kind of writing that is featured on the blogs of Gawker Media, the man behind the blog empire remains unmoved. He has always been quite clear on publishing, not what would interest a journalist, but rather what attract the regular surfer of the internet—stuff like fall from grace of popular celebrities, new Apple gadgets and sextapes. Indeed the controversial nature of content on his blogs have often landed Denton on the wrong side of the law as in the case of a extract from a leaked sextape of former professional wrestler Hulk Hogan that was published on Gawker. But Denton has almost always been unapologetic about his unabashed populism. In fact, in 2009, a memo, titled "We're Not Running a Newspaper," circulated among his employees reminded them that. "At some media organizations you might get rapped for running a premature story. At Gawker Media, you'll lose way more points for being scooped on a story you had in your hands."

With the success of Gawker, Denton tried to replicate the model in different parts of the country—he launched a blog known as Defamer to give all the gossip on Los Angeles as well as Wonkette about D.C. and later added other sites. However not all of these turned out to be popular and as a result he had to shut down some like Wonkette as well as Kinja which was a news aggregation site. At the end of the day, it is his eye for the bottomline that drives Denton and which is actually responsible for his stupendous success. He was featured at the 502nd position in the 2007 'Sunday Times Rich List', with an estimated wealth of 140 million Sterling Pounds or roughly 205 million USD based on the sale of his previous companies as well as the current value of Gawker Media.

In January 2016, there were reports of Denton agreeing to sell a minority stake to investment company Columbus Nova Technology Partners.

Denton continues to live in New York City and while for several years, he ran his blogs out of his SoHo apartment, now Gawker Media has its own address; also instead of depending on ill-paid freelancers, the company now has a strong base of salaried employees. Denton though remains as determined as ever to continue with his own brand of irreverent and dark humour—which few things on this planet can escape.

□

34

Peter Thiel

Peter Thiel is an entrepreneur and venture capitalist who has financed several successful internet startups and high-tech initiatives. An American of German origin, he has been ranked 10th on *Forbes* 2016 Midas List and enjoys a net worth of 2.7 billion USD, as of July 2016.

Early Life

Peter Thiel was born on October 11, 1967 at Frankfurt am Main in what was then West Germany. He grew up with his father Klaus Thiel, a chemical engineer and mother Susanne Thiel as well as a brother named, Patrick Thiel. The family moved to the United States when Peter was just a year old, and was raised in Foster City, California. Peter turned out to be an expert in chess and was even a US-rated Chess Master, having reached to the topmost rankings under-21 players in the country.

Thiel received his Bachelor of Arts degree in Philosophy from Stanford in 1989 and acquired a J.D. from Stanford Law School in 1992. An avowed libertarian, he founded 'The Stanford Review', in 1987 along with Norman Book. The University journal eventually gained some notoriety for challenging campus mores including political correctness and laws against hate speech.

Budding Entrepreneur

After his graduation from Stanford Law School, Thiel worked as an intern for Judge J. L. Edmondson of the United States Court of Appeals for the 11th Circuit for one year. In between 1993 and 1996, he traded derivatives for Credit Suisse Group and at the end of this period he founded a multi-strategy fund, 'Thiel Capital Management'.

In 1998, with Max Levchin, Elon Musk, and Ken Howery, Peter Thiel set about launching an online payments system known as 'PayPal' which would serve as the electronic alternative to traditional paper methods like money orders and cheques. While the basic idea was to cater to the burgeoning industry of e-commerce, the group was also motivated by the goal of creating an online global currency that would be outside the dictates of bureaucracies and governments and especially protect the currencies of people across the globe from value erosion caused by inflation. In an inspirational speech given in 1999, Thiel outlined ultimate vision saying, "In the future, when we make our service available outside the U.S. and as Internet penetration continues to expand to all economic tiers of people, PayPal will give citizens worldwide more direct control over their currencies than they ever had before. It will be nearly impossible for corrupt governments to steal wealth from their people through their old means because if they try, the people will switch to dollars or Pounds or Yen, in effect, dumping the worthless local currency for something more secure".

Despite its lofty aim, PayPal often faced challenges in the form of banking and Visa card regulations in the early years. But once these initial hiccups died down, PayPal soon became popular enough to be recognized as one of the world's largest Internet payment companies. Its success prompted eBay to acquire it in 2002 for 1.5 billion USD. In the middle of 2015, eBay decided to spin-off PayPal into an independent company. After this it went through a second

IPO on July 20, 2015, when it was accorded a valuation of 46.6 billion USD.

The other major company that Thiel has co-founded is 'Palantir Technologies', an analytical software firm which he currently heads as the Chairman and has been backed by the CIA as well.

Astute Investor

Apart from co-founding hi-tech companies himself, Peter Thiel has been a successful investor too. Right after the acquisition of PayPal by ebay, he founded a global macro hedge fund named 'Capital' which currently has 700 million USD worth of assets under management.

In 2005, Thiel became a managing partner in 'Founders Fund', another venture capital fund set up by the former co-founders of PayPal like Nosek and Ken Howery while Sean Parker, an early employee of Napster and ex-president of Facebook, joined in 2006. Based in San Francisco, Founders Fund was created to provide investments in companies building revolutionary technologies. The firm invests at all stages across a wide variety of sectors, ranging from fundamental ones like energy, health, and consumer Internet to highly specialized like aerospace, advanced computing and even artificial intelligence. In January 2005, the firm raised its first fund of $50 million from individual entrepreneurs and angel investors.

Peter Thiel in fact was one of the earliest investors in social media giant, Facebook and though he sold most of his 10 per cent stake after its 2012 IPO, he still sits on the board. Apart from these, Thiel is the co-founder and investment committee chair of "Mithril Capital Management" as well as the co-founder and chairman of 'Valar Ventures'.

Philanthropy and Other Interests

Continuing from his university days, when Thiel launched the rather outspoken Stanford Review, he has held radical ideas about progress and technology. He has thus donated vast sums of money towards projects as varied as artificial intelligence, anti-aging research and sea-steading technology. He is an ardent supporter of projects which employ highly advanced technology to better the quality of human life. To make this possible, he has come up with a series of schemes like the Thiel Fellowship, announced in September 2010, which offers 100,000 USD to 20 people under 20 years of age, if they wish to quit college to work on their own ventures.

Yet another initiative by Thiel has been the setting up of 'Breakout Labs' in October 2011 with the aim of financing early-stage scientific research that is perhaps not only too unconventional to be supported by government or traditional scientific funding bodies, but also too speculative in long-term to attract venture investors.

For all these varied achievements and contributions, Peter Thiel was honoured as a 'Young Global Leader', by the World Economic Forum in 2007, which recognized him as one of the 250 most distinguished leaders, less or equal to the age of forty, in the world.

□

35

Pierre Omidyar

Pierre Omidyar is an internet tycoon of Iranian origin who was born in France but later moved to the US. Omidyar is famous as the founder and Chairman of online auction giant, 'eBay' which is currently valued at around 27.9 billion USD. Omidyar himself enjoys a net worth of 7.3 billion USD, as of June 2016. In recent times both he and his wife have been giving away a lot of their wealth to Omidyar Network—a philanthropic initiative that was founded to support both non-profit and for-profit ventures that are committed to bring about social changes.

Early Life

Omidyar was born on June 21, 1967, in Paris, France to parents who were both successful professionals. While his mother was a doctorate in linguistics and a well-known academician, his father was a urologist. When only seven, his family moved to United States and settled in Maryland where his father accepted a residency at Johns Hopkins University Medical Center. From the time he was a young boy, Omidyar was hooked to computers—in fact he wrote his first program when he was only fourteen years old, as a way of cataloging books in the school library. In 1984 Omidyar joined St. Andrew's Episcopal School in Potomac, Maryland from where he finished high school. Owing to his interest in computers, he then enrolled in Tufts University in Medford, Somerville, Massachusetts, to study for a bachelor's degree in computer science. After graduating in 1988, he took up a job with an Apple Computer subsidiary named Claris, where he was part of the team that involved in the upgrading of MacDraw to MacDraw II. In 1991, Omidyar tried his hand at entrepreneurship when he co-founded a pen-based computing startup known as 'Ink Development'. Though it was not popular initially, after being rebranded as an e-commerce company and renamed 'eShop', it saw a moderate level of success before being acquired by Microsoft in 1996.

Success with eBay

The story of eBay starts even earlier—in the summer of 1995, Omidyar created code for a page that would enable people to list items for auction. The 28 year old creator called this 'Auction Web' and was pleasantly surprised to find out the site attracting steadily increasing number of buyers and sellers. This prompted him to set up a separate site devoted to auctions, which he named 'eBay' after discovering that his first choice of a moniker, Echo Bay, was already taken.

At the time Omidyar was working for General Magic, an Internet phone venture backed by Apple. But the increasing volume of business at eBay soon began to demand his full attention. Its revenues were made up of a nominal charges for sellers posting their auction notice as well as a small percentage of the successful sales. Omidyar thus found that the company could make money by simply setting up a place for buyers and sellers to meet online. Nine months after eBay launched its first auction, he quit his day job to devote himself full time to eBay.

While Omidyar became the Chairman of eBay, he brought in talented professionals to look into the day-to-day running of the company. Thus Jeffrey Skoll joined the company in 1996 and two years later, in March 1998, Meg

Whitman was brought in as President and CEO. She continued to run the company until her retirement in January 2008 and in the intervening years she helped eBay to continue to expand through launches in new sites like Australia, Canada, Germany, Japan and the United Kingdom as well as acquisitions and joint ventures.

The next stage of success came when eBay went public in September 1998. It had one of the biggest initial public offerings and its stock soared more than 163 per cent on the very first day of trading, making both Omidyar and Skoll billionaires. By the end of 1998, the eBay was reported to have around 2.1 million members and generate approximately 750 million USD in revenues.

In July 2015 however Omidyar stepped down as Chairman of the company after its split from former subsidiary PayPal. However he continues as a member of the board in both companies although his involvement in day-to-day operations of either company has drastically come down.

Headquartered in San Jose, California, eBay currently has an employee strength of 11,600 and figures at number 52 on *Forbes'* 2016 list of World's Most Valuable Brands.

Other Interests

Omidyar is also the founder of 'First Look Media', that he launched in collaboration with Glenn Greenwald, the former *Guardian* reporter who published government documents, leaked by the National Security Agency's Edward Snowden. First Look Media is the parent company of online newssite 'The Intercept', which first appeared online in early 2014. According to Omidyar, the venture stresses "The fundamental importance of a free and independent press", that is the bedrock of any true democratic society.

Apart from this, Omidyar is the owner of various resort properties in southern California and Mexico and has long term plans to develop resorts and homes in Hawaii.

Philanthropy

A long time resident of Hawaii himself, Omidyar is married to Pamela Wesley and the couple have three children. After building eBay to a market leader in e-commerce, Omidyar has been gradually decreasing his stake in the company and has given away a substantial percentage of his shares to his philanthropic investment firm, named the 'Omidyar Network'. In September 2015, he gave away 10 per cent of his eBay holding, valued at around $270 million in shares to the Network. In all Omidyar and his wife Pamela have donated around $327 million to their foundation and others charitable organizations in 2015, according to the Chronicle of Philanthropy.

Achievements

Today Omidyar figures at 163rd position on *Forbes* List of 2016 billionaires of the world, and has a 60th ranking in United States alone. The eBay founder and now philanthropist credits his success to the spirit of creativity and entrepreneurship as he once revealed at the November 2011 Conference of Non-profit Communities of Hawaii, with this striking question, "In Silicon Valley, we say if you haven't tried something and failed, and actually learned something from that failure, then why would I want to work with you?"

□

36

Reed Hastings

Movie buffs across the world are familiar with 'Netflix', the online movie and video rental service that has made tremendous strides in popularity ever since its launch in 1997. The brains behind this site is American internet entrepreneur, Reed Hastings, not only who co-founded the online video streaming site but as the CEO ushered in a different management culture whose influence exceeded far beyond the company and onto the industry as a whole. More importantly he revolutionized the entertainment business with a service which allowed people to watch recent movies and series from the comfort of their homes and in a cost-effective manner. As of May 2016, Hastings enjoyed a net worth of 1.32 billion USD, according to Forbes.com.

Early Life

Born as Wilmot Reed Hastings, Jr. on October 8, 1960 in Boston, Massachusetts, the future internet billionaire was the son of a lawyer who had served in the Richard Nixon administration. After high school, he enrolled into Bowden College to study mathematics and graduated with a bachelor's degree in 1983. Hastings then joined the Peace Corps and left for Swaziland to teach maths. Upon his return to America, he earned his Master's degree in computer science from Stanford University, specializing in artificial intelligence.

Budding Entrepreneur

As a software developer, Hastings' first job was at Adaptive Technology, where he invented a tool for debugging software. However after working there for around a year, he decided to start his own business. Thus in 1991 he founded 'Pure Software', which offered products to fix software problems. The company did reasonably well and it went public in 1995. Two years later it was bought by Rational Software, leaving Hastings with a substantial profit.

Success with Netflix

Hastings first got the idea of starting a different kind of video rental service when one day in 1997 he realized that he had forgotten about a rented video cassette of the movie, Apollo 13 and was left with a hefty $40 late fee. He came to the conclusion that even a gym, where one could work out as much or as little as one wished for a fixed membership, had a more practical business model. This prompted him to launch a mail-based subscription service for DVDs which was a new technology at that time. Hastings and Randolph named the service 'Netflix' and incorporated the company in 1997 and next year Hastings assumed the position of the company CEO.

From 1998 onwards the company started shipping rented DVDs to customers through mail. Initially Netflix customers could rent each DVD for a week but eventually they were allowed to rent unlimited number of DVDs against a fixed monthly fee. While customers could manage their Netflix accounts online, the DVDs were still sent and received by mail.

However all that changed when in 2007 Netflix started streaming content via the Internet. It also expanded its table of products and while it continued to offer movies and videos, eventually its service broadened to include TV shows as well as original content like Emmy Award-winning series—House of Cards.

In all this, Hastings' role proved crucial. He was primarily responsible for expanding Netflix through a strong advertising campaign as well as focusing on the company's offering of indie films, documentaries and other rarely available movies. With the arrival of technology that made streaming downloads possible, Hastings pushed for the rebranding of Netflix as a primarily online video streaming rather than a DVD subscription service. In fact Hastings tried to spin-off the company's DVD rental service into a separate entity named 'Qwikster'. However the plan backfired and the spin-off had to be cancelled.

But apart from a rare slip here and there, Hastings' leadership at Netflix has been astute. The video streaming site now has 75 million members globally and this in turn has translated to a 1.32 billion USD net worth for Hastings, according to *Forbes* data, as of May 2016.

Apart from changing the face of the entertainment business, Hastings is also known for ushering in his unique brand of management style. Netflix employees are known to be paid more than those in parallel appointments in other similar companies, though at the same time, Netflix does not hesitate to let go of employees delivering an average performance, albeit with a hefty release package.

Netflix is by no means the only business interest in Hastings' life. Since June 2011 he has been a Director on the board of Facebook and even served on the board of Microsoft from 2007 to 2012.

Interest in Educational Policies

Apart from his business, Hastings is keenly engaged with contemporary educational policy in the United States. He has not only served on California's Board of Education but is a particularly ardent supporter of charter school organizations. He believes that it is necessary to free publicly funded elementary or secondary schools from some of the statutes that apply to other public schools, so that they can work with greater degree of independence in producing certain results, which are set forth in each school's charter—these of course in return for a minimum level of accountability on the part of these schools. As part of this initiative, Hastings on occasion has publicly opposed the elected boards on grounds that school districts need to have more control over their boards.

Additionally Hastings has worked for the promotion of technology growth and innovation through his membership in 'Technology Network', which is a high-profile political network of business executives. He is also a member of the 'Giving Pledge' and recently started 'The Hastings Fund' to promote his education policies.

□

37

Reid Hoffman

Reid Hoffman is an American venture capitalist, internet entrepreneur and author. His best known venture is 'LinkedIn' which is a social media site for professional and business networking. According to Forbes.com Hoffman's net worth was 3.7 billion USD, as of July 2016.

Early Life

Born as Reid Garrett Hoffman on August 5, 1967 in Palo Alto, California, the future entrepreneur was a brilliant student since childhood. His mother, Deanna Ruth and his father, William Parker Hoffman, Jr. were aware of young Reid's potential. The boy grew up in Berkeley, California where he attended The Putney School. After graduating high school he enrolled in the Stanford University where he won both a Marshall Scholarship and a Dinkelspiel Award. He graduated in 1990, with a B.S. in Symbolic Systems and Cognitive Science.

Budding Entrepreneur

Next with the aim of pursuing a career in academics, Hoffman also studied for M.A. in Philosophy from Wolfson College, Oxford University and excelled as a Marshall Scholar. However upon earning his degree in 1993, he realized that he would have a much wider impact on society if he went into entrepreneurship. To prepare himself in the world of technology, Hoffman joined Apple Computer in 1994, where he worked on eWorld, a rudimentary form of online social network. After eWorld was acquired by AOL in 1996, he worked for sometime at Fujitsu.

Hoffman next set up his first company called 'SocialNet.com' in 1997. This was again an early version of social media site though it did not become popular as such. In the meantime, he became a part of PayPal's founding board and in 2000 joined the online payment service company as its full-time COO. In this appointment, he was mainly responsible for maintaining external relationships for the company which ranged from payments infrastructure and business development to government and legal.

Success with LinkedIn

In December 2002, Hoffman drew on his earlier experiments with social networking sites to found a company that would instead focus on professional networking over a web portal. In this way he co-founded 'LinkedIn' with two former colleagues from 'SocialNet'. The site went live on May 5, 2003 and became one of the first business-oriented online social networks in the internet. With LinkedIn, members could not only create professional profiles and connect with each other but could even invite others to become a connection, whether or not that person was also a user of the site.

For the first four years of LinkedIn, Hoffman remained its CEO after which he took on the roles of its Chairman and President, Products. In June 2009, he became its Executive Chairman. So successful was the company that on May 19, 2011, it was taken public. Hoffman too was reaping the fruits of success and with the IPO of LinkedIn, his own stake in the company became worth at least 2.34 billion USD.

Acquisition by Microsoft

The next major landmark in the fortunes of LinkedIn came in June 2016 when software giant Microsoft decided to acquire it for a staggering $26.2 billion. This all-cash deal turned out to be Microsoft's costliest acquisition till then, much larger than its 2011 takeover of Skype for which it paid 8.5 billion USD or $7.2 billion deal with which it bought Nokia's mobile phone business in 2013.

The Microsoft acquisition made Hoffman himself richer by at least 800 million USD. With the deal being priced at $196 a share, Hoffman's stake of nearly 14.5 million shares in the LinkedIn became worth around 2.8 billion USD, pushing up his overall net worth to 3.7 billion USD, according to *Forbes*.

Till November 2014, LinkedIn boasted of over 332 million members in more than 200 countries across the globe. However in the first quarter of 2016 it reported a substantial 19 per cent increase in its user base from the previous year, taking its total user base to 433 million, prompting *Forbes* to comment, "LinkedIn is, far and away, the most advantageous social networking tool available to job seekers and business professionals today".

Other Ventures

With the assets earned from LinkedIn and previous ventures, Hoffman soon emerged as one of the leading angel investors of the tech sector in United States. In 2010 he became part of Greylock investment group and was given the responsibility of heading their 20 million USD Discovery Fund. The areas of his focus here ranged from enterprise software and consumer internet to online marketplaces, payments and social networks. Among the most high-profile investments that Hoffman supervised here included Airbnb and Zynga, apart from others like Viki and Shopkick.

Among his ventures, Hoffman is also known for his early investment in the social media giant, Facebook just as he later became a member of the "PayPal Mafia", a nickname given to a group of former employees of the online payment processing company who have launched their own startups and often invest in each other's ventures. Because of his many successful and varied investments, Hoffman was ranked at the eighteenth position in *Forbes* 2016 Midas List which features the topmost investors of the country.

Other Interests

Hoffman is a prolific writer as well and has published books on internet startups, entrepreneurship and motivation. In 2012, he published *The Start-Up of You: Adapt to the Future, Invest in Yourself, and Transform Your Career* with co-author Ben Casnocha and two years later, he published *The Alliance: Managing Talent in the Networked Age* with Ben Casnocha and Chris Yeh. Apart from these, he frequently lectures at reputed universities like Oxford University, Stanford University, Harvard University, the MIT's Media Lab and other institutes of repute.

Hoffman also sits on the board of several non-profits and philanthropic organizations that focus on youth, innovation and global entrepreneurship. From 2006 to 2007 he served on the board of a non-profit initiative called 'Centre for Citizen Media'. Yet another organization which Hoffman is associated with is 'Kiva.org', a peer-to-peer online microlending service that supports low-income or disadvantaged entrepreneurs and students.

Personal Life

Hoffman is married to Michelle Yee since 2004 and the couple lives in Palo Alto, California. He is a self-confessed fan of the Strategy Board Game Settlers of Catan and has even designed a customized version of the game, named, "The Startups of Silicon Valley."

For all his achievements in business and technology sector, Hoffman has been decorated with various awards and honours-perhaps the most notable among these was the one when in April 2014, President Barack Obama named Hoffman as a Presidential Ambassador for Global Entrepreneurship "To help develop the next generation of entrepreneurs".

□

38

Ronnie Apteker

Ronnie Apteker is an internet pioneer, business leader and film producer from South Africa. He is mainly famous for launching 'Internet Solutions'—the first Internet Service Provider of South Africa in 1993 which turned out to be one of the most successful post-apartheid businesses in the country and encouraged generations of South Africans to venture into entrepreneurship.

Early Life

Born as Ronen Apteker on 19 August 1967 in Cape Town, South Africa, the future South African business leader was attracted to technology right from his student days. Not surprisingly therefore, after high school he enrolled in the University of the Witwatersrand, graduating with an M.Sc degree in Computer Science *cum laude* in 1994.

The World Wide Web had just been started in 1993 at CERN, with the original intention of allowing scientists and researchers to share information from anywhere in the world. However as the real potential of the web dawned on its creators, CERN put the World Wide Web software in the public domain, thus enabling users anywhere in the world to create websites and connect with each other on the internet.

In 1993, as Apteker and a friend from his university, Thomas McWalter, explored the new invention, its enormous potential for business became clear to them. They realized how the internet would make the process of accessing real time solutions to IT problems really simple besides opening up a global marketplace for goods and services. At the bottom of it all, Apteker knew that South Africa would have to join the internet revolution if it did not want to be left behind on the path of economic progress.

Success with Internet Solutions

With this vision in mind, Apteker convinced leading South African enterprises to incorporate the internet into their business systems and to bring this about he started the first internet service provider of the country, Internet Solutions, in 1993. Though Apteker's technological and business knowledge was sound, he found that debts were piling up. In order to get funding, Alon Apteker and David Frankel were roped into the company. Though Internet Solutions at the very beginning provided dial-up connection to home users, eventually it realized that success lay in nurturing a large corporate client base and ever since it has kept that focus. Some of its earliest clients included Price Forbes (later renamed to Alexander Forbes), Times Media (Johnnic), Sasol, Q-Data, ICL, IBM, The Argus Group (Independent Group), Sybase and such others.

From providing internet access to its corporate clients, Internet Solutions soon went on to providing them with and related IT solutions, which ranged from online banking, reservation systems and media archiving to payment gateways and complex security solutions. This consistent focus on corporate customer bases made Internet Solutions the market leader in the South African IT industry for a very long time to come.

In order to fuel his vision of further expansion, Apteker began looking for funding once again in 1996. The following year, he managed to close a deal with prime networking company, Dimension Data, selling to the latter 25 per cent of

Internet Solutions. Just a year later, Dimension Data bought the remaining 75 per cent of the company too. In return, the team of Directors including Apteker, his brother Alon, David Frankel, Thomas McWalter and Andras Salamon were paid Rand(R)300 million. Today, intent Solutions provides e-business services to more than 80 per cent of South Africa's top 250 listed companies and has over 4,500 customers.

Movie Bug

Having made millions from the sale of Internet Solutions, Apteker began looking for other interesting things to do. And what attracted his attention was cinema! In 2000, he began a second innings as an independent film producer. Among the films that he has produced are 'Material', 'Tell Me Sweet Something' and 'Cold Harbour'. Though Apteker's films have met with popular and even critical acclaim in his own country, they have been unable to find a wider popularity in the global audience.

Another aspect of the showbiz in South Africa that features Apteker's involvement is the stand-up comedy club scene. In 2002, he produced 'Laugh Out Loud'-South Africa's largest stand-up comedy TV show-which became a big hit, and even earned half a million Rand for the 'Reach for a Dream Foundation'. In fact many of the actors in Apteker's films like Riaad Moosa, Joey Rasdien and Vincent Ebrahim have come from the ranks of successful stand-up comedians in South Africa.

Apteker's love affair with the Internet, though continues. In recent times, he has started an internet-based initiative known as 'The Vottle Project'. This is a free online service that enables people to come together through a virtual marketplace, where they can buy and sell goods and services. Equally important Vottle promotes social interaction among its users as well as the promotion of grass roots arts and culture. Apteker is believed to have been inspired by Craigslist in America and started The Vottle Project with the aim of establishing a similar online community in South Africa where people could not only trade but also interact and socialize. The Vottle Project takes its community responsibilities seriously and has also added a crime watch feature using which users can report on criminal acts in their neighbourhoods.

Apart from all this, Apteker keeps busy with writing for the *Business Times* once a month on the philosophy of business. He has written several books including the *1996 Trading Spaces: Exploring Internet Solutions* as well as the more recent *Ronnie Apteker's Funny Business: The Secrets of an Accidental Entrepreneur* that released in 2010. Apteker still serves on the boards of several business committees within South Africa and continues to be associated with many charity organizations and fund-raising drives.

□

39
Sanjeev Bhikchandani

Sanjeev Bhikchandani is an Indian entrepreneur who founded the company 'Info Edge' which in turn owns the immensely popular job portal, 'Naukri.com'. Currently Bhikchandani is the executive Vice-chairman of Info Edge whose market capitalization in 2015 was almost 1.7 billion USD or Rs. 10,385 crore.

Early Life

Sanjeev Bhikchandani was born in 1964. His father was a doctor at a government hospital while his mother was a homemaker. As a child he attended St. Columbas School in New Delhi from where he finished high school in 1981. He next enrolled in the highly reputed St. Stephen's College, New Delhi where he graduated with a Bachelor of Arts degree in Economics in 1984. Then he joined one of the most elite Business schools in the country—the Indian Institute of Management in Ahmedabad, where he earned his MBA in 1989.

Bhikchandani's first job, after passing out from Business school was, in marketing at GlaxoSmithKline, which was then known as HMM. However the entrepreneurial bug had already bit him and in 1990 he convinced a friend to partner him, in the setting up of two companies—Indmark and Info Edge (India). While Indmark was supposed to specialize in pharmaceutical trademarks, Info Edge focused on producing salary surveys and reports.

The ventures turned out to be less than successes—consequently Bhikchandani and his partner decided to split up in 1993. According to the final agreement, each partner got to keep a company and this is how Bhikchandani ended up with Info Edge (India).

Launch of Naukri.com

While looking around for business ideas in 1996, one day Bhikchandani noticed that all his friends read business newspapers back to front, as the job listings were inevitably printed on the last pages. He was then struck by the lack of one single reliable source for job ads. That was also the time when the internet was just taking off in India and its commercial opportunities were as yet unexplored in the country.

Bhikchandani and his team decided to take the lead and launch an online job portal. The original site would be very basic—it would be merely a collation of job ads onto one accessible platform with the aim of attracting some customers. Over time, the team hoped that if the site could gather sufficient traffic, the companies would begin to approach them directly.

In April 1997 thus Naukri.com went live with 1,000 ads taken out of various magazines. The server was located in the United States and at the time, Bhikchandani was compelled to use the servant's room in his father's house in Delhi as his office.

Initial Challenges

Not surprisingly, the first ten years of running the business proved difficult. Bhikchandani found meeting expenses a perpetually uphill task. Later he recalled how he went without a salary for months and worked twice as hard as anyone in the company. Other ways of slashing costs were to buy second-hand computers and furniture in his office. During this time, it was his wife 'Surbhi' who stood by him like a rock and offered him the much-needed support. An alumna of IIM, Ahmedabad herself, she worked in the MNC, Nestle which gave the family a substantial salary to meet its expenses. While his wife quit her job in 1995, the next year Bhikchandani himself became the Consulting Editor of *The Pioneer's* career supplement called 'Avenues'. Best of all, it gave him a monthly cheque to fall back upon while his company was still facing teething troubles.

Growing Strength

Ten years after Bhikchandani launched Info Edge, he began to reap the fruits of his labour. Naukri.com emerged as the foremost job portal in India. Even more importantly, it became the first Internet firm to be listed on the Indian Stock Exchange when it went public in 2006.

Eventually Bhikchandani added two more portals, property search website, '99acres.com' and matrimonial site, 'jeevansathi.com' to the portfolio of Info Edge. However Naukri.com has remained its flagship property, making up for more than half of Info Edge's revenues and more than 100 per cent of the profit – indeed the profits from this job portal have helped Bhikchandani to finance other projects within Info Edge and even other businesses outside it.

One of the most high profile of Bhikchandani's investments has been the popular restaurant discovery service, 'Zomato'. Info Edge is Zomato's single largest shareholder with a 50.1 per cent holding. At first Bhikchandani pumped in 1 million USD in the site which he followed it up with five subsequent rounds of investment, bringing his funding to a total of Rs. 327 crore.

As of 2015, Zomato owed Info Edge investments to the tune of over Rs. 2,030 crore. The results show in Zomato's increasing popularity on the Internet. Every month some 30 million people visit the site, looking for restaurants and related dining options. Recently Zomato made a daring acquisition of worth 52 million USD when it took over Seattle-headquartered 'Urbanspoon', thus making its debut in the United States—the largest and most competitive market. Indeed the acquisition has given Zomato a head start in other markets like Australia and Canada.

In all, Info Edge has invested about Rs. 570 crore in various companies like Zomato, while not all of have turned out to be profitable, it had to write off around Rs. 35 crore in three of its investments—StudyPlace, 99labels and Floost—many have given ample evidence of Bhikchandani's business acumen. For example Info Edge was again an early investor in PolicyBazaar which is a portal that enables users compare different insurance products. With its 23 per cent stake in PolicyBazaar, Info Edge seems on comfortable ground as the online insurance aggregator was accorded a valuation of 100 million USD in May 2014.

Apart from online ventures, Bhikchandani also owns Quadrangle, an offline executive search business. His success seems on a rising curve. From 2014 to 2015, share prices of Info Edge climbed from around Rs. 500 to around Rs. 850, making its market capitalization more than 1.7 billion USD or Rs. 10,385 crore. Bhikchandani has won several awards for his trailblazing success in the Indian e-commerce scene like the Ernst and Young-Entrepreneur of the Year Award in 2008.

□

40

Scott Heiferman

While social networking sites have made it possible for people from across the world to connect with each other, sociologists have also pointed out a flip side to this – the unhealthy trend of online relationships replacing face-to-face relationships. For people who wish to combine the best of two methods – using the power of internet to rally people together but meeting in real life – meetup.com is a popular option. This is the brainchild of Scott Heiferman, an American entrepreneur who is best known for founding 'meetup.com', which is today the largest network of local community groups.

Early Life

Scott Heiferman was born in 1972 and grew up in Homewood, Illinois, in a large family of four other siblings. They were much older to him and already working as doctors, artists or entrepreneurs while he was still growing up. Heiferman counts this awareness of varied fields of activity as an important educational resource during his childhood.

He was interested in computers right from the beginning. When still in school, he programmed an Apple II computer, designed a Commodore VIC-20 graphics program and even worked at a Macintosh Software Company called Challenger Software.

At the same time his entrepreneurial instincts were evident too; when still a high school student, he started his first business–that of offering a local coupon package for a nearby town. Though it did not make him famous, yet it was successful enough to finance his first year in college when he enrolled in the University of Iowa to study engineering.

However eventually Heiferman graduated with a degree in business and took up a job with Sony in Montvale, New Jersey as an Interactive Marketing Frontiersman, as part of which he also designed the first online site for the company.

Soon Heiferman co-founded a photo sharing network named 'Fotolog', which became popular enough to total a billion uploaded photos by over 30 million users. In 1995 he moved to Queens, New York and launched an online ad agency known as 'i-traffic', which too became a success at the height of the dotcom boom of the 1990s. Astutely Heiferman sold it in 1999 to Agency.com before the bubble burst. For a while he continued to work with the new owners but left in 2000.

Founding of Meetup

At the beginning of a new decade, living in the Big Apple and comfortable with the funds from the sale of 'i-traffic', Heiferman still felt a lack of purpose–he even worked at McDonald's for a few weeks! But then an incident which changed the lives of millions of people in America and across the world, compelled Heiferman to sit up and take stock of his life too. The terrorist attack of 9/11 on New York City shook him out of his ennui and he felt a deep urge to connect with people around him. He wanted to get to know the people who made up his neighbourhood and community. This urgency inspired Heiferman to create a way for people in local communities to connect online and then translate this connection into real life interactions.

Another inspiration behind the founding of Meetup was the recognition that people bond better over common interests. When Heiferman decided to attend a concert by his favourite music band, Luna, for more than the twentieth time, he found few people willing to accompany him. Yet at the concert, he discovered that many who had turned up, had attended quite a few of the previous concerts as well. This set him thinking if people could be brought together to interact over common interests.

In 2002, Heiferman launched Meetup with four partners. Headquartered in New York, the site allows users to choose from a wide variety of groups–categorized according to interests, distance, community, etc.–that they can join for free. However group organizers have to pay a fee and this is the source of revenue for the company.

Growing Success

In April 2013, the portal reached an important milestone – its 100 millionth RSVP that users send to confirm their attendance for a meetup. Also according to statistics provided by Heiferman himself, meetup's new member signups increased by a substantial 40 per cent in the first quarter of 2013 while the number of its active members rose by an even higher 46 per cent. More importantly for the fortunes of the company, there was a 40 per cent increase in new groups created over the past year which translated to a respectable rise in revenue.

Currently meetup is the largest online organizer of community events in the world. It has a presence in almost two hundred countries over the globe with more than a hundred thousand groups. More than 50,000 self-organized community events, called meetups, take place every week. Nearly 13.8 million people now "use the internet to get off the internet". The success of the site is related to the fundamental need of every thriving community for support groups, play groups, hobby groups, business circles, running groups, community action groups and so on.

Apart from being the CEO of meetup, Heiferman is an angel investor in Betaworks, Founders Collective, Virgance, 20x200, and other ventures.

Achievements

On September 13, 2008, Heiferman married Emily Krasnor, an Officer for the United Nations Development Fund for Women. He has been honoured with various awards in recognition of his entrepreneurial success. In 2005 he received the Jane Addams Award from the National Conference on Citizenship and the previous year, he was named in MIT Technology Review "Innovator of the Year".

Heiferman believes that it is essential for a community to search for new ways of making face-to-face friendships–especially, in an age where people seem to prefer being glued to their smartphones over speaking with the person next to them. With meetup, Heiferman has made it his mission of connecting people in real life and thus sustain the fundamental bonds which underlie a thriving community.

□

41
Sean Parker

Sean Parker is an American internet billionaire who co-founded the popular online music file-sharing service called 'Napster'. Additionally he served as the first President of the social networking giant, Facebook Inc. As of April 2016, Parker was believed to be worth $2.4 billion, according to Forbes.com.

Early Life

Sean Parker was born on December 3, 1979, in Herndon, Virginia. His father was an oceanographer in the service of the US government who noticed and nurtured his son's interest in computers early on.

Sean's childhood was marked by poor health, as he frequently suffered asthma attacks that were at times severe enough to land him in the hospital. Often compelled to stay home, Parker turned into a voracious reader and got hooked to computers. His natural intelligence lapped up the lessons that his father gave him in computer programming on an Atari 800.

By the time he turned a teenager, Parker was proficient enough to hack into the computer networks of companies and other organizations around the world. This landed him in trouble when he was just 15, and was picked up by the FBI and directed to compensate for his illegal activities by doing community service with other teenage offenders at the local library.

Around this time, Parker came across another teen computer whiz, Shawn Fanning–the two got together and with a few others, launched 'Crosswalk', an Internet-security company that enabled clients to prevent cyber attacks. Though the business failed to take off, the opportunity helped Parker and Fanning forge a bond that would result in other business partnerships in future.

While still in school, Parker developed an early version of a Web crawler as part of a project for a state computer science fair. It was so good that his project was not only judged the best in Virginia but also brought him into the notice of the CIA, which even offered Parker an internship. However Parker declined the offer and continued to explore possibilities on the web.

Fortunes of Napster

When he was nineteen, Parker refused his parents' suggestions of going to college and instead teamed up again with Fanning to launch an online music sharing service which came to be called 'Napster'. Within just a few months of going live, the site started attracting millions of users from across the world. While such popularity brought success to the founders, it also brought in opposition from the music industry over copyright issues. Eventually after a lawsuit filed by the Recording Industry Association of America in 2001, Napster was ordered to be taken down. At the same time, Parker himself had fallen out with his team members at Napster and was forced to leave the company, taking refuge with friends by turns. This turned out to be the lowest point in his life when he found himself broke and without a home.

Soon though the 21 year-old Parker got his act together and teamed up with other entrepreneurs like Minh Nguyen, Todd Masonis, and Cameron Ring to launch 'Plaxo', a contact management startup. This was designed as an online service that kept users' address books up-to-date and drew on the potential of the emerging wave of social networking over the web. Here too Parker was unable to get along with the company management and decided to quit in 2004.

Facebook had been just launched at that time by Zuckerberg and his team. Not surprisingly Parker was attracted to this new site and the enormous potential for social networking as well as business that it promised. He encouraged Zuckerberg to dropout of Harvard to devote himself to building Facebook full time. More importantly Parker played a crucial role in obtaining funds for Facebook from PayPal co-founder Peter Thiel as well as the venture capital firm Accel Partners. In return, 24 year old Parker was made the first President of Facebook by a grateful Zuckerberg. Though Parker held the positions only briefly, it proved to be the source of the bulk of his future fortune.

Encouraging Startups

In 2006 Parker joined the Founders Fund, a venture capital firm co-founded by one of PayPal's founder Thiel. In his role of a managing partner here, Parker led the Fund's investment in Spotify in 2010. This was a Sweden-based digital music service which offered home computer users free access to its music library and on a paid subscription basis to users on mobile devices. In exchange Parker was offered a seat on Spotify's Board. Parker's support to Spotify was crucial in enabling the service expand its presence in the American digital music market and in the process challenge the dominance of Apple's iTunes store.

On his own, Parker also founded the 'Brigade Media', in 2014 as a way of using the power of social networking to accelerate political engagement by people.

In recent years, Parker has been very active in funding political candidates and charitable causes. In June 2015 he launched 'The Parker Foundation', giving 600 million USD to startups working in life sciences, global health and civic engagement. In November 2015, the foundation donated an additional $10 million to establish a new autoimmunity research lab at the University of California, San Francisco. Previously, Parker had given funds worth $4.5 million to the University to fund the fight against malaria and $24 million to Stanford University to set up an allergy research center. Parker has been a strong advocate of legal marijuana use by adults and for this; he has pledged $500,000 if a proposed initiative in California is approved by voters in 2016.

Personal Life

Sean Parker's colourful whimsical personality is proof of how he likes to live on his own terms. In the movie 'The Social Network', which dealt with the founding of Facebook, his character was played by popular singer and actor, Justin Timberlake.

In the summer of 2013, Parker tied the knot with Alexandra Lenas in a lavish Lord of the Rings themed ceremony. According to media reports, Parker had ordered theme-based attires for himself, his bride and even for the three-hundred and more guests who had been invited to the exotic affair, held in a Big Sur hotel's backyard filled with gorgeous redwood trees. However the event attracted the attention of California's state regulators who fined Parker 2.5 million USD for tampering with the forest setting. To Parker typically, the controversy became more than a simple legal issue and an example of how in today's world of social media, privacy and reputation are fraught with danger.

42
Sergey Brin

From a Russian immigrant family to the richest person in the US-Sergey Brin's story reads no less than a fairytale. But then the transformation he and Larry Page brought about into the world of internet was no less than magical. The creation of Google search engine has revolutionized the way an ordinary user uses the World Wide Web and along with the array of products and services, Google has now launched, the company has emerged a giant player in the world of technology. According to *Forbes* List of February 2016, Brin today is one of the three people jointly listed as 11th richest in the world, with a net worth of 39.2 billion USD.

In the Beginning

Born as Sergey Mikhaylovich Brin on August 21, 1973 in Moscow, Russia, the future internet entrepreneur was the son of Russian Jewish parents, Yevgenia and Mikhail Brin. Because of their ethnicity, they decided to migrate to the US in order to escape the growing persecution of Jews in Russia during the 1970s. Thus young Sergey arrived with his parents in the US he was when only six years old. Since both his parents were graduates of Moscow University, his father became a professor of mathematics at the University of Maryland while his mother became a researcher at a NASA Space Center. The family's academic background was a valuable resource for Sergey during his childhood. His inborn genius for mathematics and research was well honed by his parents who were also careful to teach him his mother tongue.

Young Brin joined the elementary school at Paint Branch of Montessori School in Adelphi, Maryland after which he studied at Eleanor Roosevelt High School in Greenbelt, Maryland. In September 1990 Brin enrolled in the University of Maryland, from where he graduated with a Bachelor of Science in 1993 with honours in computer science and mathematics. After this, he earned a graduate fellowship from the National Science Foundation with which he began his graduate study in computer science at Stanford University. In 1993, he interned at Wolfram Research, the developers of the well-known symbolic mathematical computation programme, 'Mathematica'.

Budding Entrepreneur

While studying at Stanford University for his doctorate, Brin came across Larry Page, another computer science graduate. The two hit off intellectually and agreed to work together on a research project titled "The Anatomy of a Large-Scale Hypertextual Web Search Engine", wherein Brin focused on data mining. While working on the problem of measuring the importance of a given web page based on the backlink data gathered by a web crawler, they developed an algorithm called 'PageRank'. This made use of new kind of technology that analyzed the relevance of the backlinks that connected one web page to another. Brin and Page realized the immense potential of this algorithm for building a web search engine far more advanced to the ones that already existed.

To transform their ideas into reality, Brin and Page bought several cheap computers and installed them in the dormitory rooms at Stanford University. After months of hard work, in August 1996 they came up with a simple search engine, which general internet users could access as well, though at the time, it was still on the Stanford University website. It was still named 'BackRub' and worked by entering a query to which it provided a list of backlinks ranked by importance. By mid-1998 their search engine began getting around 10,000 hits a day and then the pair finally realized the huge potential of what they had created.

Launch of Google

But for the commercial development of their search engine Brin and Page realized, they had to incorporate a company. The two began borrowing from family, friends and acquaintances and managed to raise around 1 million USD. With the funds available, they rented a garage in Menlo Park and placed some servers here so that they could begin working. Around this time, Andy Bechtolsheim, the co-founder of Sun Microsystems, contributed another 100,000 USD which eventually helped the two and they officially incorporated their company as "Google, Inc"–thus named for the mathematical term "googol". The immense popularity of the Google search engine made the company a huge financial success and turned both Brin and Page into billionaires almost overnight. Since then, Google has launched many new products and services, taken over several other internet companies like YouTube and entered into partnerships with other corporations to become one of the fastest growing internet companies in the world.

During the time of Google's founding, Brin served as the President of the company while Page became the CEO. In 2015 Google underwent restructuring and a new parent company 'Alphabet' was founded in which Brin currently serves as the President.

The Man Behind the Success

Despite his meteoric rise, Brin never entirely forgot his origins. In the summer of 1990 when he accompanied his father and a group of high school math students, on a two-week exchange program to the Soviet Union, Brin realized the enormity of his parents' decision to leave the country and he is believed to have said to his father, "Thank you for taking us all out of Russia."

In 2007, Sergey Brin married a biotech analyst named Anne Wojcicki. An ardent supporter of health information initiatives, Wojcicki convinced Brin to found a company together, named "23andMe", which is committed to research about the human genome project. In 2008, a son was born to the couple and three years later they had a daughter. However in 2013, Brin separated from his wife and two years later in June 2015, they finalized their divorce.

Another initiative close to Brin's heart is the fight against Parkinsons's disease with which his mother, Yevgenia has been diagnosed. In 2008 thus, he decided to make a donation to the University of Maryland School of Medicine, where his mother is being treated. In fact Brin used the services of 23andMe, to find out more about the condition. He was told that although Parkinsons is generally not hereditary, both he and his mother possess a particular mutation of genes that raises the possibility of developing the condition in later years. In an attempt to ward off the condition, Brin exercises rigorously and in fact has taken up a variety of high-adrenaline sports in recent years. These range from roller hockey and ultimate frisbee to gymnastics, springboard diving, and even high-flying trapeze. Indeed the media often reports stories of him arriving to meetings in rollerblades. Even in his office at the famous Googleplex headquarters, he is most often seen in his workout clothes and Vibram FiveFingers barefoot shoes. In fact, Brin at times walks around on his hands, much to the awe of his colleagues and employees!

Life Beyond Google

Apart from developing the Google search engine with Page, Brin has been busy with many other ideas for innovation. Since 2012, he has been involved with the "Project Glass", program which seeks to develop an augmented reality head-mounted display so that users can experience hands-free display of information and even interact with the internet through natural language voice commands. Yet another project that Brin is passionate about is the Google driverless car whose ultimate aim is to make robotic cars available to the general public. Using "artificial intelligence," based on video cameras and radar sensors, such cars can drive themselves and hopefully cause fewer accidents. In June 2008, in an effort to develop space travel for general purposes, Brin invested $4.5 million in Space Adventures, the only company that sends tourists to space. No wonder then Brin is often called the "Renaissance Man" of today's world. With his creative genius and innovative he is ideas firing up different kinds of projects, Brin recalls the legendary inventive minds of the Renaissance Period like Leonardo da Vinci and Galileo.

Sergey Brin has been honoured with several awards and titles for his achievements and innovations. In 2002 he received the MIT Technology Review "TR100" and in 2004 he was awarded with the "Marconi Foundation Prize", regarded as the Highest Award in Engineering. The same year he was honoured with the "Academy of Achievement's Golden Plate Award" and inducted into the National Academy of Engineering for "Leadership in development of rapid indexing and retrieval of relevant information from the World Wide Web."

□

43
Simon Nixon

Price comparison sites are some of the most frequented destinations on the internet. They come in handy not only to decide which product to buy but to get a good deal too. And 'moneysupermarket.com', is one of the most popular of such sites. It was co-founded by British internet entrepreneur Simon Nixon who became a billionaire with its success. In March 2016, he sold off the last of his stake in the company, which made him richer by £124 million. Even till a year before, he enjoyed a net worth of 1.44 billion USD.

Early Life

Born as Simon Justin Nixon on August 19, 1967, in Stamford, Lincolnshire, the future tech entrepreneur attended school at St Richard Gwyn Catholic High School in Flint. In a 2008 interview to *The Telegraph*, Nixon revealed that he was motivated to become an entrepreneur by his uncle who was a successful businessman, "My early inspiration was my uncle who had his own business and was very successful. From a young age I wanted that kind of success and it inspired me to start my own business. I didn't have a business mentor however."

With this aim in mind, Nixon joined Nottingham University to study for an accountancy degree but quit before completing it, as later claimed that he found the subject "boring".

Budding Entrepreneur

Upon leaving college, Nixon started his own mortgage consultancy. He next started a magazine where all mortgage products with best buy tables were listed so as to help advisors. This was spun off into 'Mortgage 2000', a mortgage sourcing and packaging company.

Nixon however was on the lookout for something with greater impact and when Freeserve launched free internet access in 1999, he saw his chance. With Duncan Cameron, he launched 'moneysupermarket.com' in 1999, initially to help users compare mortgage deals but eventually it expanded to include a wide variety of financial services and products like credit card and personal loan information.

In June 2007, Cameron exited the business and sold his 47 per cent stake to Simon Nixon for £162 million. Just the next month the company went public and was listed on the London Stock Exchange, riding high on a market capitalization of £843 million. At the same time Nixon released £101 million and took over 54.5 per cent of the business.

In 2012, Nixon took over 'Moneysavingexpert.com', which then became part of moneysupermarket.com. The company has often been in the news for its catchy TV commercials that frequently feature pop singers and popular actors.

Recent Career

In recent years, Nixon has been winding up his association with moneysupermarket.com. In 2013 he moved to Jersey citing his desire to live in a sunnier climate, especially in the wake of a particularly wet British summer in 2012. However critics saw in this, an attempt to save taxes on capital gains, as by that time Nixon had already began offloading his shares in moneysupermarket.com.

Nixon had already stepped down from the position of CEO at moneysupermarket.com in 2008 but had continued to play an active role as executive chairman. Eventually he moved on to a less active role as non-executive deputy chairman. At the end of 2015 he stepped down from the position of non-executive deputy chairman too and in December the same year he sold some of his shares in the company which brought him £98 million payout. After this however he was prohibited from selling any more shares until the firm had reported its full year results on March 1. In March 2016, Nixon sold off his remaining shares in moneysupermarket.com for £124 million, thus bringing his total earnings from selling his stake in the company to more than £700 million. Also in 2016, energy regulator Ofgem concluded an investigation into price comparison websites to decide whether they were in breach of competition law. The end to this controversy brought in some good news for the site, as it was suffering from a decline in stock value in the wake of impending exit of Nixon.

Other Interests

Apart from business, Nixon's interest range from travel and sports like squash and jogging to healthy cooking and property. In fact, it was the last interest that prompted him in 2003 to buy a beautiful Grade II-listed Georgian residence in Sandown Terrace, Boughton overlooking the River Dee. Though in 2013, before his relocation to Jersey—he had claimed that he would never sell his Chester home, as that is where he had his family and friends, eventually though he decided otherwise and in August 2015 he sold his Chester home for £1.5 million.

Nixon's success as an internet tycoon in the United Kingdom has been well recognized. In 2008, he ranked at the top of The Telegraph's "Made It by 40", list as the richest young entrepreneur in Britain. Even after five years later, *The Sunday Times,* Rich List of 2015 claimed that Nixon was worth a staggering £945 million, making him the 120th richest person in the UK.

REFERENCES

1. http://www.telegraph.co.uk/finance/markets/2954737/Simon-Nixon-UKs-richest-young-entrepreneur.html

□

44
Steve Jobs

No compilation of the foremost digital entrepreneurs of this age can be complete without a bit on Steve Jobs. Inventor, innovator and businessman-Steve Jobs revolutionized the way people communicate and access information. According to US Registry Records, he filed no less than 346 patents but he is especially remembered as the brains behind game-changing inventions like the Apple personal computer, Macbook, i-Pod, i-Pad and of course the i-Phone which not only forced the mobile phone industry to shake off its lethargy and innovate but in fact changed human trends in communication, recreation, commerce and information.

Brief Biography

Born as Steven Paul Jobs on February 24, 1955 in San Francisco, California, the future inventive genius was actually given up for adoption after his birth, as his biological parents were a pair of unmarried graduate students and did not want a family right then. He was adopted at birth by Clara and Paul Jobs and the family later moved to Mountain View, California where Steve grew up.

Right from his earliest childhood, it was clear that Steve was no ordinary boy—he was extremely quick in learning and eager to explore. In fact, he had already learnt to read from Clara before even starting to school. As a child, Steve liked nothing better than to help his father tinker with electronics in the family garage—the two would spend hours taking apart and reassembling televisions, radios and stereos.

At school, Steve quickly learnt all that there was in the curriculum and moved way ahead of his classmates. As a result he was often bored and ended up playing pranks on other students. In fourth grade, he was tested and his score turned out to be that of a high-school sophomore level.

Soon Jobs left for Oregon where he enrolled in Reed College to study. But that old restlessness grew stronger and just after six months, he dropped out.

Fascination with Computers

After travelling for seven months which included a trip to India, Jobs zeroed in on what he wanted to do with his life-computers. Describing his reaction to the first computer terminal he laid eyes on, Steve later said, "I fell totally in love with it." In 1970, a mutual friend introduced Jobs to Steve Wozniak and two hit it off right away. They started making a computer, working out of Jobs' garage and in 1976 created 'Apple I'. This was the first modern personal computer from the ordinary person's perspective. Before the existence of Apple, computers were sold not as assembled machines but in kit form.

Soon Wozniak came up with ideas for an improved version and Jobs convinced investors to put in funds for the 'Apple II'. Their joint endeavour, in which Jobs created the design and Wozniak focussed on the technology, was a big success and ushered in a new age of personal computers. In 1984, Jobs launched the 'Macintosh' computer and this in turn changed the whole computer industry. It became the first popular computer with GUI. This did away with the need to remember commands and their syntax. With its powerful operating system and its smooth windows and icons as well as a mouse to move between them, one could now control the computer by just pointing and clicking. Furthermore its GUI made possible the creation of programs such as 'PageMaker' and 'Photoshop'-apps that would revolutionize publishing. Then there was its 'MacPaint' software which enabled ordinary computer users to access digital art.

As soon as the personal computer became a familiar fixture, Jobs being the innovator, had to do something better. He ended up inventing the 'iMac' in 1998. It was the first legacy-free personal computer which no longer featured floppy disks. Instead of expansion cards, it had provisions for USB connections. Also it was built for easy internet use since Jobs rightly foresaw how enormously popular the internet would become for sharing of information, entertainment, business and communication.

In the meantime, Jobs had also bought the computer graphics division of Lucas Films and this would mark the birth of the world-famous, 'Pixar Animation Studios'. Eventually he would go on to invent a whole range of personal devices like the 'i-Pod' and 'i-Pad'. Though music lovers across the world already had their walkmans and mp3 players, Jobs went ahead and invented the iPod. The previous devices lacked in aesthetics and convenience, which i-Pod had in spades. Combined with clever marketing, the i-Pod soon became the personal music device of choice. Finally came the 'i-Tunes' store from where users could easily download music too. This, the business model with Apple providing the player, the software and the shop, went on to rake in millions of dollars for Jobs and his company.

Innovations Galore

But what transformed the technology industry was the i-Phone that Jobs announced in January 2007. Jobs designed this as a single device that would integrate the functions of varied devices such as mp3 players, GPS navigators, cameras and even the personal computer with the mobile phone. The individual technologies like icons, touchscreens and gesture control already existed but disparately. What he did was to come up with a sophisticated operating system which would integrate all these capabilities into a single terminal. This was the iPhone operating system which later came known as 'iOS', the operating system that would go on to power the iPhone, iPad and iPod Touch. Most of all, the iPhone's striking good looks ensured that the customer could never go back to the boxy Blackberry or the chunky Nokia. In this way, iPhone became a game changer for the global smartphone market. Finally in 2008, with the launch of iPhone 3G, Jobs propagated the idea of buying smartphone apps from a single central digital store. With the device already fitted with a powerful operating system and great graphics, now the store offered a free software development kit (SDK) which led to a deluge of apps and that continues even now.

But Jobs was still not done. Even after the iPhone swept the market, he began designing a new device and the result was the iPad which was announced on January 27, 2010. This portable tablet became a success mainly on account of its latest iOS operating system as well as its fantastic Apps. Though the original iPad was only available through Apple stores or its website, still it sold a whopping 300,000 units on the very first day. In the meantime Jobs filed patents to safeguard several of i-Phone features and in October 2013-after his death—Apple got the right to protect many details of the original iPhone. Thanks to its continuing massive sale across the world, Apple is now the world's richest technology company.

Personal Life

As an individual, Jobs touched the highs and lows of a born genius. While he amazed the world with his innovation and creativity, some people also found him obsessive, finicky and difficult to work with. However most employees were extremely loyal because he knew how to motivate them. In public his image acquired also mythical proportion fuelled, as it was by reports of Apple's enormous financial gains as well as his own appearance-indeed the man in round horn rimmed glasses and black turtleneck sweater became an icon for creative success in popular culture.

At the same time Jobs was rather secretive about his personal life. He was married to business executive Laurene Powell, for more than 20 years. The two were married in a small Buddhist ceremony in Yosemite National Park in 1991. The couple had three children—Reed Paul, Erin Sienna, and Eve and the family lived in Woodside, California. In 2003 Jobs was diagnosed with pancreatic cancer and after a long battle with the disease which also included a liver transplant, he finally died of complications on October 5, 2011.

All his inventions and innovations are ample proof of the creative and business whiz that Steve Jobs was. His biggest successes were not inventions from scratch but masterpieces of reinvention as he himself said, "Innovation distinguishes between a leader and a follower."

Fortune magazine named him as the "Greatest entrepreneur of our time"—one who not only excelled in coming up with the perfect technology and design but who could tap into what the user wanted and then delivered something far better.

□

45
Stewart Butterfield

Stewart Butterfield is an internet entrepreneur from Canada who is best known as the co-founder of popular online photo-sharing service, 'Flickr'. He later founded 'Slack', a team messaging application. Butterfield enjoyed a net worth of 1.64 billion USD, as of 2016.

Early Life

Butterfield was born in 1973 in the rural outpost of Lund, located in the Canadian province of British Columbia. Stewart's family lived in a log cabin during the earliest part of his childhood and till he was three, the place was not even equipped with running water. When he was five, his parents moved to Victoria and soon Stewart was presented with a computer. The young boy couldn't get enough of it and while still in school, Stewart learnt coding on his own. In college, he began to design websites for others and in the process even earned some money.

In 1996 Butterfield graduated from the University of Victoria with a BA in philosophy and after two years earned his Master in Philosophy from the world famous University of Cambridge.

Budding Entrepreneur

One of the earliest jobs that Butterfield took up after

leaving University was at a startup called Gradfinder.com which had been launched by a friend, Jason Classon. But then the dot com bubble burst and the two were compelled to sell the firm which despite the troubled times, managed to make some profit.

Success with Flickr

In the summer of 2002 Butterfield teamed up Classon and his new wife Caterina Fake to launch yet another venture named 'Ludicorp'. Based in Vancouver, this developed a multiplayer online role-playing game called 'Game NeverEnding', but was unable to find a suitable buyer. Instead Butterfield exhorted his team members to focus on a particular feature of the game that might have some potential for popularity. This was an online photo-sharing service that eventually came to be known as 'Flickr'. It was unveiled before the world in April 2014 at a talk that Parker was scheduled at an O'Reilly conference called Etech in San Diego on certain aspects of NeverEnding like REST, RSS and API. However all these were also features of Flickr and as Butterfield finished the demo, the tech world was blown over by the new photo-sharing service.

Butterfield and his team lapped up the success that Flickr brought their way, including the proceeds from the sale of Ludicorp to Yahoo! in March 2005. In 2006, he was named in the "Time 100", *Time* magazine's list of the 100 most influential people in the world, and also appeared on the cover of *Newsweek* magazine. Butterfield remained as the General Manager of Flickr for another three years until he left Yahoo on July 12, 2008. This exit also marked the breakup of the husband and wife team as Butterfield and his wife too parted ways.

Other Ventures

In 2009 Butterfield co-founded a new company called 'Tiny Speck' which set about developing another massively multiplayer game. The result was named 'Glitch' which was launched on September 27, 2011. However the game was unable to attain much popularity and though it had to be closed down as a business, Tiny Speck agreed to make its creative aspect available under a Creative Commons License.

One fallout of Tiny Speck's misadventure with Glitch was the development of a new chat-based communication tool within the company. Butterfield once again spotted potential where others saw only failure and in August 2013 he gave a preview of this communication service, known as 'Slack'. This instant messaging service was publicly released in February 2014 and by August the same year, it boasted of more than 120,000 registered daily users along with a revenue of 1.5 million USD. Not surprisingly the company began attracting investments and in 2015 venture capitalists Kleiner Perkins and Andreessen Horowitz agreed to pump in a whopping $340 million into the young company which was valued at 2.8 billion USD.

In 2015, Butterfield was honoured as the, "Wall Street Journal's Technology Innovator for 2015" and the same year, he was awarded TechCrunch's Founder of the Year Crunchie. Slack is now universally recognized as among the fastest-growing apps on the internet. In less than two years since its public launch, Slack grew to a major company with more than 180 employees and 25 million USD in annual recurring revenue. Many of the global tech majors like eBay, Sony, Nordstrom, PayPal and the New York Times are already using Slack and more are sure to follow in the days to come. Butterfield himself shares this optimism and believes that the time when Slack will largely replace office email, is not very far away.

□

46

Tom Anderson

Much before Facebook took over the world, internet users had their own social networking space to share music and connect with their favourite bands. This was 'MySpace' that was founded in 2003 by Tom Anderson and Chris DeWolfe which became exceedingly popular in the decade of the 2000s. As of 2015, Anderson enjoyed a net worth of 60 million USD.

Early Life

Born as Thomas Anderson on November 8, 1970 in Santa Monica, California, the future internet whiz was fiddling with computers from an early age. In fact he was hooked to computer hacking as a pastime and once even broke through the security of Chase Manhattan Bank–a move which prompted a knock on the door from the FBI though young Anderson was not charged as he was just fourteen years old, at that time.

Eventually however he grew out of his wild ways and went to college. Incredibly none of the courses he studied had anything to do with computers. In 1998, he earned a bachelor's degree in rhetoric and English from the University of California, Berkeley while in 2000 he completed a master's degree in film from the University of California, Los Angeles. However, this interest in arts went to influence his career in important ways–while still studying at Berkeley, Anderson became the lead singer of a band called "Swank" and eventually it drew him to founding 'MySpace' which was originally planned as a social networking site for music lovers.

While still working at his master's degree in film studies, Anderson joined a digital storage company named Xdrive in 2000 and started working as product tester and copywriter in order to earn some cash on the side. Though the company went out of business next year, he met DeWolfe here–an association that would have a significant impact on his future and career.

Birth of MySpace

Anderson and DeWorth met each other while working at Xdrive but when the firm went bankrupt, the two friends decided to start a direct marketing company titled 'ResponseBase' which was eventually sold to Brad Greenspan's eUniverse in late 2002.

However by that time, the germ of the idea of a social networking site was well in the minds of Anderson and DeWorth and together with other employees of eUniverse, the first pages of MySpace went live in August 2003. According to an anecdote, part of the impetus came from strict membership rules of a similar site called Friendster which blocked accounts of users who did not give their real names. Anderson was determined to counter this and in response pushed for the creation of MySpace with its more relaxed membership policy. Soon, the founders had to set up a company in order to run MySpace as a business and thus 'InterMedia' was founded.

Anderson eventually became popular as the public face of MySpace. This was in large part due to the fact that every newly created MySpace account would automatically get Anderson as a default "friend". Soon Anderson began to be known as "MySpace Tom" and sometimes even ended up as the butt of jokes in media and popular culture.

Life after MySpace

However in 2009, both founders exited the management of MySpace–incredibly at a time when MySpace was bigger than even Facebook. Anderson moved on to explore other interests. In keeping with his lifelong attraction for the arts, he took up photography and in September 2014 a interview to ABC network elaborated: "I'm not necessarily trying to represent nature exactly. I'm trying to make something beautiful like a painter would."

□

47

Chris Dewolfe

Chris DeWolfe is famous as the co-founder of 'MySpace'. With Tom Anderson, DeWolfe created this highly popular social networking site which in turned helped the latter to reach a net worth of 50 million USD, as of 2015.

Born in 1966, Chris DeWolfe studied at the Lincoln High School and then completed his graduation from the University of Washington in 1988, where he was also part of the prestigious, 'Beta Theta Pi Fraternity'. Later he went on to get an MBA from the University of Southern California. In the final year of his college, DeWolfe took a course titled, "The Impact of Tech on Media and Entertainment," and this set him thinking how the internet could be used to bring music fans and performers together. In fact, as part of the paper that he was supposed to write for the course, DeWolfe created a networking programme titled, "Sitegeist". This included aspects of online classifieds like 'CitySearch' and 'Match.com', along with the messaging function of IM. Not only did DeWolfe get an "A" for this project but more importantly it became the source of inspiration for the creation of MySpace in 2003 that he co-founded with Tom Anderson.

According to some trend-watchers, the success of MySpace as a social networking site and also the sale of this increasingly popular site to News Corporation in 2005 for a whopping 580 million USD was large due to DeWorth's entrepreneurial foresight. DeWorth was the CEO of the company while Anderson its president. During this time, MySpace emerged as the most popular social network, with over 135 million worldwide unique visitors a month–even ahead of its main competitor Facebook. Also DeWorth was instrumental in giving MySpace its unique association with music. Its MySpace Music section was especially influential as it enabled fledgling artists to post their music for free–in fact the site can be credited with launching the careers of several famous musicians like Lily Allen and Sean Kingston. In all these ways, MySpace brought about far-reaching changes in the music label industry.

Even after leaving the management of MySpace in 2009, De Worth agreed to remain as strategic adviser to MySpace and serve on the board of MySpace China. Eventually though, he gravitated to other business ventures. Together with Aber Whitcomb and Colin Digiaro—his former employees of MySpace he purchased a social gaming platform, 'MindJolt'. With the acquisition of two more companies–'Hallpass Media', a free online gaming network and 'SGN', a mobile games company, MindJolt became a major player in the multi platform game developing business and changed its name to Social Gaming Network in February 2012. Next year, it became even larger with the takeover of Mob Science, a video game developer. Most recently the company bagged an investment amounting to 130 million USD from Netmarble Games, the top South Korean mobile games publisher.

□

48
Tony Hsieh

Who knew that you could make millions in shoes! That is exactly what Tony Hsieh has done and that too, on the internet. American billionaire Hsieh is the founder and CEO of 'Zappos', an online retailer of shoes and apparel. Despite being expected to study for a PhD by his Taiwanese immigrant parents, Hsieh struck out with his entrepreneurial skills and started his online venture. Later he also founded 'LinkExchange', an internet adverstising network, that he sold to Microsoft in 1999—all of which has brought his net worth of 840 million USD, as of 2016.

Early Life

Tony Hsieh–pronounced 'Shay'–was born on December 12, 1973, in Illinois but later his family moved to San Francisco Bay area of California where he grew up with two younger brothers, Andy Hsieh and Dave Hsieh.

After completing school, Hsieh enrolled into the Harvard University to study for a degree in computer science–to some reluctance from his parents who wanted him to become a lawyer or doctor. Hsieh's entrepreneurial skills were evident right from his college days when he took up the challenge of running the Quincy House Grille at the campus. He would not only sell pizzas from his dorm room but also make numerous contacts, some of which would prove to be useful at a later date–like his frequent customer, Alfred Lin, who would go on to become the CEO and COO at Zappos and Sanjay Madan, with whom he would found LinkExchange.

Budding Entrepreneur

After graduating from Harvard in 1995, Hsieh took up a job at Oracle but found the corporate environment so stifling that he could not continue beyond five months. Hsieh left Oracle and started working on an internet advertising network with his former college mate Madan who had also joined and left Oracle, much like Hsieh himself. The result was 'LinkExchange' which was launched in March 1996 with the aim of enabling users to advertise their sites by putting up banner ads on other members' websites. As the CEO, the responsibility to make the LinkExchange work was squarely on Hsieh's shoulders. Though the first 30 clients were roped in by direct emailing webmasters, in the next 90 days, the site grew to the extent of having over 20,000 participating web pages and its banner ads displayed more than 10 million times. By 1998, the site had expanded considerably–it now boasted of more than 400,000 members and could claim to have a daily rotation of 5 million ads. Not surprisingly LinkExchange caught the attention of software giant Microsoft which lapped up the company in November 1998 for a considerable sum of $265 million.

With part of the money earned from the sale of LinkExchange, Hsieh next turned investor. He teamed up with his former college mate, Alfred Lin to start an incubator and investment firm, creatively named 'Venture Frogs'. In fact, according to an interesting anecdote, the firm got its wacky name as part of a dare–apparently a friend betted that if they could name their firm Venture Frogs, she would invest all she had in it. Though Hsieh and Lin accepted the dare, the friends has yet to keep her side of the bargain!

World at his Feet

In 1999 a younger entrepreneur, Nick Swinmurn,

reached out to Hsieh with what at the time seemed a bizarre idea–selling shoes and that too on the internet. According to an interview given later by Hsieh, he almost deleted Swinmurn's voicemail till he heard that "Footwear in the US is a $40 billion market, and 5 per cent of that was already being sold by paper mail order catalogs,". This caught Hsieh's attention and he agreed to pump in 500,000 USD through Venture Frogs into the Swinmurn's site that was then known as 'ShoeSite.com'.

However with Hsieh's involvement, things began changing soon. Firstly it was given a new name, the much catchier, 'Zappos', after zapatos, meaning "shoes" in Spanish. Also two months after investing Hsieh joined Zappos as the CEO. Revenues jumped from $1.6 million in 2000 to $1 billion by 2009. So successful did Hsieh's brand become that the retail giant Amazon.com acquired it on July 22, 2009, for around 1.2 billion, USD, leaving Hsieh richer by at least another $214 million.

Hsieh however remains involved in the day-to-day running of Zappos.com from downtown Las Vegas. In fact after 2009, he embarked on an ambitious project to revive downtown Las Vegas which had long been bypassed in development plans, in favour of the Strip. Initially Hsieh envisioned the Downtown Project as a place where employees of Zappos.com could work and live as well. But with time, the project expanded to include the techies and other entrepreneurs of the local area who preferred to live and work there.

Also Hsieh has been known to put an innovative management culture at his company. Dubbed "Holacracy", this does away with a hierarchical structure of authority and instead places all employees at the same level, who are then encouraged to work at specific tasks and as part of defined 'circles'. Additionally a fun and quirky atmosphere is nurtured at the workplace with the view that this promotes creativity and productivity.

Other Ventures

In 2011, Hsieh joined the board of JetSuite which designs and manufactures ultra-light jets. Hsieh's investment, in fact, enabled JetSuite to go for two new Embraer Phenom 100 jets. These, like the large commercial jets, possess a twin-engine, two-pilot system and comparable safety features but weigh less than 10,000 pounds and thus, are highly fuel efficient.

Hsieh has taken to writing in recent times and in order to share his entrepreneurial skills with the world, wrote a book titled *Delivering Happiness*, released in June 2010, the book quickly shot up to the top of the New York Times Best Seller List and continued to figure on the list for 27 consecutive weeks. Additionally it was profiled in many globally reputed publications, like, The Wall Street Journal, The Washington Post, CNBC, The Huffington Post and TechCrunch. In recognition of his business success in the world of e-commerce, Hsieh was honoured with the "Ernst and Young Entrepreneur Of The Year Award", in 2007.

□

49
Vikas Malpani

Vikas Malpani is an Indian internet entrepreneur, best known for founding 'CommonFloor.com', an online real estate site that enables users to browse through property that they wish to buy or rent. Currently Malpani is the head of CommonFloor Groups, the apartment management section of the CommonFloor site that caters to the requirements of apartment residents.

Early Life

Malpani was born in Gujarat, a state in the western part of India in the year 1985. After completing school from his home state, he enrolled in the Visvesvaraya Technological University, Bangalore from where he graduated with a degree in Computer Science Engineering in 2006. His first job after graduation was with SAP labs, where he worked on the NetWeaver mobile team.

Success with CommonFloor

The regular day job however could not retain Malpani's interest for long and he planned to start his own enterprise. Soon he met two other promising entrepreneurs, Sumit Jain and Lalit Mangal. The three decided to launch CommonFloor.com while MaxHeap Technologies became the founding company. The online portal CommonFloor.com was intended to cater to a user's all round residential requirements, starting from the search of an apartment to facilitating interactions within an apartment community and even connecting to relevant service providers.

The idea behind CommonFloor.com came to Malpani and his team as they found significant gaps in the market. While there were some sites to provide information about properties on sale or rent, these rarely helped in the subsequent process. As such, there existed gaps in communication amongst the owners, buyers as well as members of residents' association in the large housing societies. In order to address these failings, CommonFloor.com was designed as a single-stop portal not only for connecting home-seekers to apartment owners but also with agents, dealers, residents, association members as well as service providers.

After the launch of the company, Malpani took upon the responsibility of its day-to-day running. Starting from the initial sale to campaign management and then from campaign execution to product management, he was involved in almost every step of the way.

Currently, Malpani oversees CommonFloor Groups which is a division of CommonFloor.com offering online apartment management solutions to housing societies. Contemporary living in apartments is vastly different from living in small towns and single house neighbourhoods of earlier times. Nuclear families living in apartments in new cities often have to contend with unique challenges that become difficult to resolve on their own. It is here that online portals like CommonFloor.com steps, since as they offer a range of technology products and services solutions to cater to various needs related to living in an urban housing society. What's more, these are easily integrated on web and mobile apps and require no extra cost.

CommonFloor.com has proved to be a boon not only for individuals living in apartments but for residents' associations too, since it offers administration tools that promote better interaction between residents and the association, software to manage accounts and thus brings down maintenance costs. Apart from all these the website also provides information on important subjects such as laws and taxes relate to property besides promoting general awareness about these matters among readers.

With his hard work and perseverance, Malpani has brought about the growth of CommonFloor.com which is now not only used by apartment owners and residents but also associations and property managers of the societies. In 2012 the service had a presence in 105 Indian cities. As many as 28,000 communities-constituting more than 2,500,000 houses were listed with it. Malpani and his team are now planning to expand the reach of CommonFloor.com and its software beyond Indian shores to Singapore, U.S., UK, UAE, and Africa as well.

In 2012 Malpani was featured in the List of "35 Entrepreneurs Under 35", released by prestigious Massachusetts Technology Review.

□

50
Vikrant Bhargava

One of the few internet entrepreneurs of Indian origin to have tasted global success, Vikrant Bhargava is the co-founder of 'PartyGaming', an online casino operator and the owner of the widely popular online Party Poker. A former credit officer at the Bank of America, he is believed to have been the brains behind the emergence of online casino gaming as a popular online recreation and the success of PartyGaming, in particular. According to *Forbes*, Bhargava enjoyed a net worth of 870 million USD, making him the 30th richest Indian in 2015.

Early Life

Vikrant Bhargava was born on 14 December 1972 in Jaipur, Rajasthan in the western state of India. He is an alumnus of Indian Institute of Technology, Delhi from where he earned his Bachelor's Degree in electrical engineering. He followed this with a business management degree from Indian Institute of Management, Kolkata. After graduating from business school, Bhargava held several positions including that of a business analyst in the business development division of British Gas as well as that of a credit officer at Bank of America. While working at Bank of America, Bhargava was given the task of managing credit exposure and revenue for valuable portfolio of corporate clients.

Success with Party Gaming

In 2000, Bhargava joined iGlobalMedia as marketing head and took on the challenge of revamping it into a popular gaming company. It became famous for launching 'Party Poker', which later turned into the world's most popular poker site. Even at that time an online casino site was not an original idea since in the early 2000s there was already a website called Paradise Poker. Encouraged by its success, Bhargava and his team thought of trying out something similar.

The challenge, of course, lay in attracting customers to an online gaming site and more importantly maintaining its credibility. It is here that Bhargava proved his mettle. He decided to launch the company in a spectacular manner and announced an online poker tournament with a first prize of 1 million USD. At the time such enormous amounts could only be won in the very biggest tournaments at actual bricks-and-mortar casinos, like as the annual World Series of Poker in Las Vegas. However such places were out of reach for most people since the entry fee for the main event would be as high as $10,000. Instead with Party Poker, more number of people could afford to enter the online tournament.

At the core of Bhargava's successful marketing plan for PartyGaming was the idea of hosting a series of online mini-tournaments with small buy-ins after which the qualifiers could be filtered to just a hundred. For the finals, these hundred would be invited on a cruise ship to the Caribbean where they would compete for the big prize money.

Though PartyGaming lost about $500,000 on the event, the tournament went a long way in attracting attention of potential players across the world. More important, it established the credibility of PartyGaming as a company which was certain to pay up to the winner. As Bhargava shared in a later interview to the *Guardian*, "We put 100 people with their partners on a cruise ship to play in a live final... because that was the only way people could really believe that a new company had paid out $1 million in first prize. It was good PR and showed the credibility of our company."

Bhargava's next strategy in popularizing Party Poker was to make use of the explosion of the game on US television in early 2000s. The World Poker Tour was telecast live on TV in April 2003. This was helped by the trend of Hollywood celebrities like Ben Affleck and Nicole Kidman playing in a tournament which resulted in a television audience of 13 million. PartyGaming too jumped the bandwagon and signed up celebrity Mike Sexton to promote its online poker site. Bhargava says in the *Guardian* interview, "People were discussing it at work and so on, and wanting to play the game having seen the TV programme, and we got the word out that if you do participate in an event like this you can do so online. We saw our market share go up from 20 per cent to 50 per cent in a fairly short period."

Among other techniques that Bhargava applied to increase the popularity of Party Poker was to make use of time-tested internet marketing techniques, like giving incentives to outsiders who brought in new players to the site. Such affiliates ranged from current players to other websites and even hundreds of online poker bloggers.

In June 2005, PartyGaming went public on the London Stock Exchange and the initial offer price of 116pondo indicated a company valuation of £4.64 billion or 8.46 billion USD. At the time Bhargava held a 15 per cent stake which was roughly worth £450 million.

In the 2005 Guardian interview Bhargava revealed that during peak hours, the number of people playing Party Poker often crossed 70,000, which was quite incredible, since two years back the figure was fewer than 2,000. The site makes money by charging a small fee from each pot in the poker win.

PartyGaming is headquartered in Gibraltar, as the existence of the Wire Act in the United States forbids gambling across state lines. This makes it dangerous for the company to be listed in America. The company's operations are ably supported by a 1,000-strong call centre in Hyderabad in India.

Though Vikrant Bhargava left PartyGaming in 2006, he continues to hold an 8.6 per cent stake in PartyGaming which along with other assets helped him to be included among the 84 Indians who featured on *Forbes* 2016 list of World Billionaires. Currently he maintains interests spread over a wide range of media, internet and philanthropic ventures.

REFERENCES

1. https://www.theguardian.com/technology/2005/mar/19/business.onlinesupplement

□

Conclusion

Many analysts feel that the digital revolution which has transformed human activity, life and community, is yet to come to a close. Many exciting things are still taking place in the world of e-commerce and information technology (IT). The range of smart appliances that can sense user requirements and fulfil them without the latter's active intervention as well as the development of artificial intelligence are some innovations very likely round the corner. Yet another trajectory has been exploring ways that can improve quality of human life–whether by developing cleaner energy and related technology or by helping users bond better with their fellow beings over shared interests, images, videos, entertainment and so on. And spearheading such innovations are dynamic entrepreneurs eager to explore opportunities and push the limits of technology in making the world a better place to live for all.

□□□